PHOEBE'S HOUSE
A Hearst Legacy

A Pictorial History of
HACIENDA DEL POZO DE VERONA
CASTLEWOOD COUNTRY CLUB
OLD HEARST RANCH

PLEASANTON, CALIFORNIA

Carole MacRobert Steele

LUMINARE PRESS
WWW.LUMINAREPRESS.COM

Printed in the United States of America

Cover Design: Claire Flint Last
Cover Photo: Hacienda del Poza de Verona as it looked at the turn of the century showing the vast amount of landscaping befitting a grand estate,which was accomplished by famed botanist Luther Burbank.
Photo courtesy Wikimedia Commons and University of California at Berkeley/Bancroft Library.

Luminare Press
438 Charnelton, Ste 101
Eugene, OR 97401
www.luminarepress.com

LCCN: 2016940253
ISBN: 978-1-937303-93-8

To my parents, Dr. & Mrs. Robert L. MacRobert.
They loved living the good life.

CONTENTS

PREFACE

PHOEBE HEARST WAS A WOMAN OF MANY CONTRADICTIONS. For everything she was, she wasn't; and for everything she wasn't, she was. Through the decades, volumes have been written about her. It's not my intention to write in depth about her life and accomplishments, but rather to paint a picture of how her life experiences and personality were reflected in the development and completion of her beloved Hacienda. Her home represented the person she was and all the things she cherished. This is a history of her home, and to describe it accurately, readers must understand the woman who rambled around its ninety-two rooms for more than two decades.

My own history with Castlewood Country Club was my motivation for wanting to chronicle its history. In addition, I've amassed a large collection of vintage postcards depicting the Hacienda through all its eras, thus providing me with some of the photographic images needed to tell its story. In the last one hundred years, this landmark has lived four lifetimes: as Phoebe's Hacienda, as a dude ranch, and twice as a country club. Although the buildings have been gone for decades, their history needed to be documented.

My father, in the carefree days of the 1950s, bought a membership to Castlewood Country Club. He was a physician in nearby Hayward, and belonging to a country club was a status symbol. Several of Dad's friends were members, and some lived in homes on Castlewood Drive. Dad considered the membership as an opportunity for our family to spend leisure time together. For my older sister and I, this meant Saturdays or Sundays playing in the Club swimming pool, which was about the only activity available for kids. My parents had never been golfers, but they soon realized they needed to learn this sport if they were going to be members of this mostly golf-oriented club. Dad even ended up winning a trophy playing in one of Castlewood's coveted tournaments. While the men golfed, the wives entertained themselves playing bridge or enjoying lunch in the dining room that overlooked the fairways. This tradition of eating lunch and playing cards is still carried on by the ladies of Castlewood.

Because it was a thirty-minute drive from our home in the East Bay, we didn't frequent Castlewood very often, but every time we did, it was fun and memorable. Driving from Castro Valley on the freeway, Dad took the Foothill Road exit, which became a two-lane road. Time passed pleasantly as we drove through sprawling farmland and rolling hills. To access Castlewood Drive, Dad made a right turn from Foothill Road. As this narrow approach twisted and turned up the hill, we passed elegant homes owned by the wealthy. These impressive homes lined both sides of the street, some with the golf course practically in their front yard. We couldn't help but be envious. Tall palm trees graced both sides of the meandering road as it narrowed into a single lane leading to Castlewood's clubhouse. On the left side of the raised causeway, a steep, bush-covered slope led down to the sparkling blue waters of the swimming pool, just as it does today. Manicured lawns and several varieties of shade trees surrounded the Olympic-size pool. Directly adjacent to the pool was the Spanish-style poolhouse with its architecturally appropriate red tile roof. The freshly mowed first-hole fairway was immediately visible on the right, seeming to stretch on forever into the horizon. At age six, I hardly knew what golf was, nor did I care about it. Through the eyes of a child, it all seemed so glamorous and opulent. I felt dwarfed by the looming size and magnificence of the buildings and landscape. In my young life, I'd never seen such a place! Now in my sixties, I wish my memories were clearer. I do remember the lobby area with its patterned carpeting, richly upholstered antique furniture, and the reception counter near the front door.

To start our day of fun, my sister and I laid down our beach towels at our favorite spot near the cement steps on the slope leading to the shallow end of the pool—these steps still exist. From this grassy knoll, Mom had a good vantage point to keep an eye on us playing and splashing in the water. A lifeguard was always on duty, often yelling at the children in a stern voice, "No running around the pool." Dad swam with us a few times, but most of the time he golfed while Mom sunned herself. She never got in the pool; she just dangled her toes in the cool water. Mom must have packed us a lunch as I have no memories of getting food from the poolhouse snack bar. What I do remember is walking up to the snack bar counter with a nickel in my little hand and asking for a Milky Way candy bar. I was delightfully surprised when the attendant handed me one that was frozen! I'd never experienced the challenge of biting into a frozen candy bar, and, to this day, I still love Milky Way bars.

I fondly remember the time when my Dad took me to the dark and dimly lit Celebrity Bar where he bought me my first Shirley Temple drink, a mixture of ginger ale, a splash of grenadine, and garnished with a maraschino cherry. The grenadine gave this special kids' cocktail its fascinating red color. In the middle of the afternoon the bar wasn't crowded with adults and I felt like a very special little girl sipping my drink in a grown-up atmosphere. The Diego Rivera mural, which filled the entire wall behind the bar, added a special ambiance to the room.

For additional recollections of fun times at Castlewood, I had to tap into my sister's memory. She is now seventy. She recalled Easter egg hunts that were held on the fairways behind the poolhouse. Dressed in our Sunday best, complete with

Modern-day photo of Castlewood Country Club's Olympic-size pool and Spanish-style poolhouse. Some remodeling has been done over the years, but both are basically unchanged from author's childhood memories. Poolhouse retains its original 1930s dressing rooms. The magnificent weeping willow tree that stood stately behind the poolhouse is long gone, its delicate branches once covering most of the red-tiled roof. The large cement steps on the grassy slope are visible at the shallow end of the pool. This is the area where author spent most of her family fun time.

Easter bonnet and white cotton gloves, we attended the annual egg hunt. It was a chaotic scene as dozens of excited children scampered among the trees and bushes in search of the elusive, brightly colored eggs. Prizes were given to kids who found the most eggs. For added authenticity, a person dressed in a bunny costume handed out candy to wide-eyed and eager youngsters. My sister remembered being thirteen and inviting a girlfriend for lunch at Castlewood and charging the meal to Dad's account. Near the lobby area, they dined in one of the courtyards that was enclosed by wrought iron fencing. Surrounded by lush tropical foliage, they sat at an ornate cast iron table. Shaded by a colorful umbrella, they were able to eat and watch all the activity happening below at the swimming pool.

In the 1950s and 1960s, my parents attended several dinner dances at Castlewood. I loved watching Mom "dress to the nines" as she put on her pink lace party dress, mink stole, and finest jewelry. Earlier in the day she had carefully applied bright red polish to her nails. With a final spritz of French perfume, she was ready to go!

Castlewood Country Club official membership card showing a 1965 expiration date. Author's father, R. L. MacRobert, M.D., was member #801. Signed and issued by the Club secretary.

This era came to an end in 1966 when Dad decided not to renew his membership. My sister and I were teenagers and no longer interested in going to Castlewood on the weekends. Since Dad didn't golf enough to warrant the Club dues, he sold his membership.

In the late 1960s, the drive to Pleasanton was still enjoyable, but the valley was growing rapidly with subdivisions crawling up the once barren hills. When I was eighteen in 1966, I drove an out-of-town friend to see Castlewood hoping he'd find it interesting and awesome. In the summer of 1969 I was living in another part of the state and heard the news that Castlewood had burned to the ground. Saddened and shocked, my first thought was, "How could something like this happen?" Forty years would lapse before I saw Castlewood again. My elderly mother was left alone when my Dad passed away in 2000. Since she hadn't seen Castlewood in several years, my sister and I decided that a ride to Pleasanton would be enjoyable for her. I'd never seen the new clubhouse built in 1972, so I was also excited for the visit. Driving the familiar entrance causeway, it felt strange seeing the new clubhouse where the Hacienda once stood. As we roamed the grounds and toured the clubhouse, I felt oddly detached. Too many years had passed.

Writing this book, I feel the same sadness. I wish I could once again see the old

Hacienda the way it was before the fire, but I'll have to be satisfied with only faded memories. On recent visits in the last few years, I'm thankful the original pool and poolhouse haven't changed much. I was hit with a wave of nostalgia as I walked down the cement steps to the pool just as I'd done sixty years ago. Images of my childhood came to mind as I looked at the same grassy slope where I'd rolled out my towel, ready for a day of fun in the sun.

There would be no fond memories to look back on if it weren't for George and Phoebe and their vision for the land. He bought the property, she built the Hacienda … and, today, Castlewood Country Club is carrying on their legacy.

Author's Notes

In the first section of the book, her name appears as Phebe until the spelling is changed to Phoebe. I kept the latter through the rest of the story since that became the official spelling of her first name.

Since it's the main subject of the story, I chose to capitalize Hacienda to keep it dignified and important.

The word Club and Ranch are capitalized, which signify Castlewood Country Club and Old Hearst Ranch.

Direct quotes from people or articles are written exactly as the originals, without corrections to grammar or punctuation.

Research on this project was frustrating at times with conflicting dates and facts in many of the resources I studied. I have tried to be as accurate as possible, and I take responsibility for any errors that may have occurred in the writing of this book.

CHAPTER 1

THE BEGINNINGS
OF A LEGACY

UNLIKE THOSE THOUSANDS OF PEOPLE BORN INTO THE HUMBLENESS of farm life in rural America, Phebe Elizabeth Apperson was fated to achieve greatness and wealth in her lifetime. Born December 3, 1842, in Franklin County, Missouri, she was named after her Aunt Phebe. Her parents were born of hearty Southern stock. Her mother, Drucilla Whitmire Apperson, hailed from Virginia, and her father, Randolph Walker Apperson, was a proud son of South Carolina. From the time she was a child living on the Apperson family farm, Phebe was a bright and tenacious little girl who loved to study and learn. Since reading was her favorite activity, books were cherished possessions. Books stimulated the visions she had of a world far beyond her small-town existence. Her imagination must have run wild with thoughts of the adventure she yearned for and the possibilities of what life had to offer. Little did she realize that in a few short years her dreams would come true.

Phebe adored children and longed for the day she'd have some of her own. When she was old enough, a local French family hired her to be a governess and tutor their children. From this experience, she learned to speak, read, and write the French language. Years later, when she made several trips to Paris, knowing French proved very useful to her. When she felt it was time to move on to other experiences, she easily transitioned from her tutoring position to becoming a primary grade teacher in the local one-room schoolhouse.

Although they lived a rural lifestyle, Phebe's parents raised her to be a cultivated and well-bred young lady. She acquired an appreciation for music from years of taking piano lessons. This structured upbringing proved most beneficial in the decades ahead as she blossomed into a grand lady of society and a woman who would play a major role in the history of the United States. Although pretty, but not beautiful, Phebe was beginning to catch the eyes of young men who were taking notice of her as a well-rounded young woman. An unlikely man who took an interest in her would end up being the one who would fulfill her dreams. He arrived in the person of George

George Hearst
1820 – 1891
Courtesy of Wikimedia Commons. Photographers Edouart & Cobb.

Phebe Elizabeth Hearst, the attractive young woman George Hearst married in 1862.
Courtesy of Library of Congress LC-USZ62-113288.

Hearst, a close friend of the Apperson family. At age twenty-six, he was several years older than Phebe. When she was a three-year-old tot, he had playfully carried her on his shoulders. Little did he realize at the time that someday he'd actually be interested in her as a mate. It was rumored that George was once in love with Phebe's mother. Drucilla was four years older than George when he asked her to marry him. She turned down his proposal, but it was not because of their age difference.

George Hearst was born in Missouri in 1820 to a rich farming family in Meramec Township, Franklin County. George was not a loafer, having graduated from the Franklin County Mining School in 1838. He was an adventurer at heart, and in 1850 he traveled to the California goldfields to seek his fortune. He was more successful in 1860 when he became one-sixth owner of the Comstock Lode, the largest producer of silver in the United States. He eventually became an owner in the Homestake copper mine in South Dakota, the Ontario silver mine in Utah, and the Anaconda copper mine in Montana. These were some of the largest and richest mining discoveries in the history of the United States. George was respected and well-liked by his peers and gaining an eminent reputation across the West as a very capable mining analyst. He was a muscular, outdoor-loving man whose favorite activities included hunting, horseback riding, and raising race horses. Gruff and coarse on the outside, he was the complete opposite of sweet, petite, and refined Phebe. He had a preference for bourbon, poker, and tobacco. She was cultured and liked to be social while he hated parties and dressing in fine clothes. Standing a mere five feet tall and weighing one hundred pounds, Phebe was the image of daintiness. Abundant dark curls fell softly around her china-doll face, her creamy complexion the texture of porcelain. Her blue-gray eyes saw George as nice looking, with a bearded face, but not a handsome man. He stood before her not particularly well dressed. Besides the physical appearance, what did they see in each other? He was hoping to find someone who would be a wife, companion, and a woman to bear his children. She was seeking a life better than what rural Missouri had to offer. She once referred to her home state as "miserable country." They were both willful, headstrong people, but he softened when he was around her.

George had become fabulously wealthy from his mining investments, and money was not a problem. He could give Phebe anything she wanted ... and he did! He was ready to marry, and, despite all their differences, George eagerly asked nineteen-year-old Phebe Apperson to become his wife. She accepted his proposal without hesitation. Her family was apprehensive about the marriage, believing that she could have chosen a better mate. Defying her parents, George and Phebe eloped soon after George's ailing mother died of cancer. The year was 1862, and the ceremony was performed by a Presbyterian minister in a private home in Steedman, Missouri. No one from either side of their families attended the informal occasion. There are no photos of the wedding, but a studio photo does exist showing Phebe possibly wearing a wedding dress and veil. It's unclear whether they were truly in love, or just able to give each other what they were each lacking in life. Phebe once declared, "If I married for money, then I got it!" Throughout their entire married life, they had great respect, admiration, and loyalty for each other. With his vast wealth, George was able to provide Phebe will all the material things she needed and the life she always dreamed of. In ways she could only imagine, her life would prove to be more satisfying—not in monetary wealth, but in the satisfaction of giving back to the people.

Immediately following the wedding, the newlyweds sailed on a steamer bound for San Francisco. Though pregnant and miserable during the voyage, Phebe was overjoyed when she gave birth to a son who would be her only child. William Randolph Hearst was born in 1863 at the Stevenson House, a family hostelry where they'd been living since their arrival in San Francisco. The baby was named after his paternal and maternal grandfathers. Phebe fondly referred to her son with names such as: little Willie, Will, Sonny, and my dear boy. George's pet name for him was Billy Buster, but as an adult people referred to William as W. R. Phebe desperately wanted more children, especially a girl, but because of the difficult pregnancy and delivery, the doctor advised against having another child. Her ability to have more children may have been hampered by the fact that George was gone for months at a time attending to mining ventures and land speculations.

San Francisco was the first place the Hearst family lived after leaving Missouri, and California ended up being the place where all of Phebe's childhood dreams came true. After several moves within the city, they finally settled in an elegant house on ritzy Russian Hill. Phebe was getting a taste of the life she always wanted. While George was away on business trips, she began to change from being a plain farm girl to becoming a fancy socialite wearing lace, pearls, and curls. She was not a snob, but at times she put on airs of grandeur. Her level of sophistication broadened as she visited local museums, galleries, and attended operas and musical events. She continued her study of French, and she was introduced to well-known artists and writers. She learned to live with George's lengthy absences and concentrated on raising her young son in a manner of her own choosing. In the end, William would disappoint her in many ways.

While Phebe entertained and made herself well-known in San Francisco social circles, George was rekindling his interest in politics. In 1865, he was elected to the California State Assembly. This was the beginning of an era that in 1887 would take him to Washington, D.C., as a senator representing the State of California. When his Virginia City, Nevada, mines threatened to fail, George started buying up thousands of acres of prime California land at sixty cents an acre. In 1865, he purchased 48,000 acres of rolling hills in San Luis Obispo County that he named La Cuesta Encantada, the "Enchanted Hill." It is known today as Hearst's Castle.

In 1873, when Willie was ten years old, he and Phebe traveled to Europe aboard the grand Cunard liner *Adriatic*. This was their first trip and it would last twenty months. George had no interest in joining them, so he stayed behind to tend to his business and political duties. Phebe wrote him several letters expounding upon their sightseeing adventures, and she kept him up to date on William's growth. She ended her letters by telling him how much she missed him and lovingly signed them "Puss," his favorite pet name for her. Endless free time and wealth allowed Phebe and Will to stay abroad for several months touring the countries of England, Ireland, Scotland, Germany, Italy, France, Switzerland, Holland, Belgium, and Austria. They hired a private tutor who traveled with them so that Will could keep up with his school lessons.

Phebe had a natural eye for beauty, and she wanted to instill in her son the same passion she had for art, architecture, and all things beautiful and historic. In a letter to George, she wrote, "He has a mania for antiquities; pool old boy." Mother and son absorbed all the best that Europe had to offer. Although only in her late twenties, it was gratifying to have an unlimited amount of money to buy rare paintings, hand-carved sculptures, tapestries, rugs, glassware, and china. In a letter George wrote to Phebe, he told her to: "Spend as much money as is necessary for your pleasure and not think of it." She could buy whatever she wanted … and she did! It occurred to her that she may never have the opportunity to travel abroad again, so she felt the need to buy while she could. At least this was the excuse she told herself. As it turned out, in the next thirty years she would travel to Europe several more times.

Phebe was fortunate that her son loved the same things she did. This pampered and protected ten-year-old boy was leading a privileged life. His mother fussed over him constantly. Part of him must have yearned for normalcy: to go to school everyday, have friends his own age, and a home with familiar surroundings. Willie adored his mother, and this early training in Europe would make him the person he'd become, one of the world's foremost collectors of art objects. Years later, his vast collections would be housed in his "castle" at San Simeon. Will gained an accrued appreciation for antiquities as he and his mother continued to explore castles, palaces, and museums. Most young boys would have their minds on other things, but Phebe's love of all things beautiful was making an impression on her son. Perhaps he was also taking notice that, although she was not a snob, having made acquaintances with European royalty, she started to avoid associating with "common" Americans who were not of her own class in life. In 1874, they sailed home where they looked forward to the arrival of several crates filled with the elegant glassware, fine china, and lavish linens they'd purchased in Europe. Also to arrive on the docks at San Francisco were dozens of pieces of art bought while on their shopping sprees. In 1880, the Hearsts bought a house on Van Ness Avenue in San Francisco. This purchase put them on "millionaire's row," as it was commonly referred to by locals. Her European purchases filled this home. Years later, Phebe would sell this home, writing in a letter to Will, "How I hate to live in San Francisco." How could she say that about the city where her dreams had been realized? She may have been missing the simplicity of country life.

George was always searching for land to purchase. In 1886, while exploring the hills of nearby Alameda County and "just looking around," he located 500 acres of ranch land in the Livermore Valley, thirty-five miles from San Francisco. Neglected and forgotten, the ranch bordered the Rancho el Valle de San Jose, a Mexican land grant owned by the Bernal family since 1839. Part of this purchase included the Alisal Rancheria on which 125 Ohlone Native Americans lived. The Ohlone were allowed to continue to live on the land, but in 1914, all their homes burned to the ground in an accidental fire. The settlement was totally abandoned by 1916. The hills and valleys teemed with wildlife, making this a perfect spot for a hunting lodge. On this land, George could relax and experience the things that brought him the pleasures of outdoor life. In the hills surrounding Pleasanton, he picked a spot to build his lodge, which would later become the site of Phebe's permanent home. Breeding and raising racehorses were among his other passions and Pleasanton had become nationally known for its racetrack and horse breeding. The ranch would provide him a place to pursue this sideline while still being able to live near the racetrack.

In 1887, having always been active in politics, George was elected by the Democratic Party as a senator from California. For Phebe, this meant a move to Washington, D.C., as a senator's wife. She disliked the public spotlight, but she was obliged to support him and remain by his side. George would have been satisfied living in a hotel, but Phebe demanded that they live in a mansion so she could fill it with her European treasures. It was during this time that she honed her hostessing skills, becoming well-known among Washington's political elite. She was referred to by Washington newspapers as an "arbiter of unsullied elegance."

George hoped his grown son would make a career in the mining business, but Will's interest lay in the *San Francisco Examiner*, a newspaper his father had purchased in 1880. George bought the newspaper to help "give a voice" to the Democratic Party. He knew nothing about running a newspaper, nor was he interested in it. Phebe would have preferred that Will go into ranching or mining, but not the newspaper business. After Will pleaded with his father, promising that he'd do a great job, George relented and let him run the *Examiner*. Ironically, on March 4, 1887, the day George was sworn in as a senator, Will was named as editor-in-chief, promising his father that he'd turn what had become a business failure into a roaring success. Residing in an apartment in the Hearst Building in San Francisco, twenty-four-year-old Will continued to live the high life on his parent's money even though he hated being financially dependent on them. He was dating "questionable" women, which greatly alarmed and disappointed his mother. All of his young adult life she'd tried to control who he dated, hoping he'd marry a well-bred and cultured young woman. A regular

This portrait of William Randolph Hearst, age 31, hangs at the far end of the Gothic Study at Hearst Castle, San Simeon, California. It was painted by family friend Orrin Peck in 1894, just before William left to start a new life in New York City.

"stage door Willie," he persisted in pursuing chorus girls.

In 1889, while the Washington, D.C., mansion was being remodeled, Phebe and a friend journeyed to Europe and Russia. It was on this trip when she became very interested in archeological museums. Fascinated by the subject, archeology became a big part of her philanthropic life, and she donated money for excavations, explorations, museum buildings, and displays. Once back home in Washington, D.C., and living in the refurbished mansion on New Hampshire Avenue, she arranged for two railroad cars of household goods to be shipped from her San Francisco home. As a result of visiting royal places and meeting royalty, she now desired to live like a queen. Newspaper articles of the day wrote that she sought to be the leader of popular society in Washington, D.C., so she set out to accomplish this by hosting elaborate gala events at her home. Each day her Victorian home was filled with the fragrance of freshly cut flowers. Rooms were not adorned with common brick-a-brac, but instead with rare and priceless ornate furnishings and art objects. The fireplace was not brick; it was made of Mexican onyx. Carved statues and busts sat regally upon marble-top tables. Phebe at long last had the home of her choosing in which to showcase her treasures. Every piece had a story, and she loved telling her guests the history behind each one. Acting as a tour guide, her guests followed behind as she led them from one awe-inspiring room to another.

To commemorate George Washington's birthday, the first of many masquerade parties was held at the Hearst mansion. Guests stepped from their carriages clad in elaborate Colonial era clothing. Phebe spared no expense; the flowers alone cost $25,000. Being an intellectual, she continued to entertain and give parties, preferring to be in the company of cultured people rather than with "social butterfly" types. Her esteemed guests included individuals possessing talent and notoriety in the world of art, music, and literature. Phebe wanted to stand out from the crowd at her parties, so she frequently wore satin brocade dresses trimmed in antique lace, her shoulders draped in ermine or sable, and her neckline adorned with rubies and glittering diamonds. Money was so plentiful that she could easily afford lavish clothing and jewels. Her household budget was $5,000 a month, which less fortunate people would find horribly shocking. George continued to spend like the affluent man that he was, his wealth coming from the buying and selling of mining stocks and real estate. He easily spent upwards of one million dollars a year.

Even with all this money, Phebe was unhappy with certain aspects of her life. She tried to stay healthy, but she suffered from "woman" ailments, headaches, and muscular rheumatism. During those times when she was feeling poorly, she must have been pleased to read newspaper accounts that she "maintained her slender figure, her

370. *Examiner Building, San Francisco, Cal.*

The Examiner Building, also known as the Hearst Building, as it looked when William R. Hearst was the San Francisco Examiner *newspaper editor. Completed in 1911, it replaced the original building, which was damaged in the 1906 earthquake. Located at Third and Market Streets, it remains today as a historical structure in San Francisco history. The Hearst family continues to conduct business from this building.*

Phoebe Hearst, in approximately 1895, during her years as a socialite in Washington, D.C., and wife of Senator George Hearst. Throughout her life, she often posed for pictures wearing strands of pearls at her neck, possibly a gift from her wealthy husband. Courtesy of Library of Congress LC-USZ62-70333.

creamy complexion, and her dark shining hair." At least the rest of the world thought she was looking well even if she didn't.

Unfortunately for George, money could not buy health. In 1890, he was diagnosed with cancer, a virtual death sentence. Years of hard living and bad habits had caught up with him. Phebe was in denial about his prognosis, believing that the power of the mind could heal the body. She tried to keep the news of his dire condition private, but speculation about his probable death began to buzz around Washington. Possible successors to his Senate seat were being discussed in hushed whispers behind closed doors. George fought bravely against the cancer ravaging his body, but finally accepting his fate, he told a reporter, "I do not fear to die. I only regret leaving my family and good friends who have been with me." William stood by vigilantly as his father lay on his deathbed in a coma, and Phebe bravely held tight to his hand as he quietly passed away. The year was 1891, and forty-eight-year-old Phebe was now a widow. Never again would she hear him call her Puss.

They had been complete opposites—the beauty and the beast—but what they had in common was the love they had for their son. Phebe disliked mining towns, politics, and horse racing, and George disliked polite society. Good men, in her eyes, were clean, well-dressed, educated, traveled, reliable, and attentive, all of which George was lacking. With loving memories of him not far from her mind, she closed up, but did not sell their home at 1400 New Hampshire Avenue. She would not remain the woman she was; she would mature into the woman she was destined to be. Her return to California would be short-lived. During this time of transition and new direction, she opted for a name change, a different spelling of her first name. Years before George died, a friend told her of a fictional character named Phoebe with an "o," indicating that maybe there was some special refinement attached to that spelling. Since Phebe sought refinement, the name change seemed appropriate and attractive. Her earliest signatures had been Phebe Hearst, or P. E. Hearst, and by 1879, it was sometimes Phebe A. Hearst. After George's death, her signature became Phoebe A., or Phoebe Apperson Hearst.

George's estate, estimated between eighteen and twenty million dollars, was left entirely to Phoebe. As parents, they agreed that Will was careless with money, and they made the decision to leave him out of the will. Through no fault of his own, he'd seen his parents live a lavish lifestyle, buying whatever they wanted or needed. He'd grown up in luxury and had been given an exorbitant monthly allowance. No wonder he never learned to be frugal; he was truly born with a sterling silver spoon in his mouth. In addition to the money, Phoebe inherited millions of acres of land her husband owned in the United States and Mexico. It would now be her responsibility

The five-ton sculptured wellhead William R. Hearst purchased in Verona, Italy, in 1892. It remained the namesake centerpiece of Hacienda del Pozo de Verona until Phoebe's death in 1919. The intent of its placement in the courtyard was for it to be the first thing guests saw when they entered through the gates of the grand estate. "These portly medieval wardens guarding the massive iron-studded entrance door admonish the visitor to bring no cares of the modern world through this ancient gateway to arcadia." Photo courtesy of The Art Institute of Chicago, Ryerson & Burnham Archives, Historic Architecture and landscape Image Collection, Mrs. Phoebe Apperson Hearst Residence.

to control and manage the extensive mines in South Dakota, Nevada, Montana, and Utah, all of which George had been a major owner. These mines were his greatest source of wealth, and he trusted Phoebe to manage them prudently after his death.

With all this responsibility on her shoulders and worrying about her playboy son, her health began to suffer. In 1892, one year after George's death, another trip to Europe was just what she needed for rest and distraction. She took her niece, Anne Apperson, as her traveling companion. Anne was like the daughter she never had. Together they sailed to Germany, France, Spain, and England. Whether by land or sea, they traveled in a style of luxury reserved only for royalty. That same year, William and his girlfriend, Tessie Parker, along with a male companion, also traveled to Europe. While visiting Verona, a tourist town in northern Italy, Will's discerning eye spotted a five-ton, beautifully sculptured wellhead in the center of a courtyard. Verona was well-known for its artistic heritage. Circular in shape, this fifteenth century wellhead was used by the women of the village to draw up buckets of water to their second story apartments. The buckets were hoisted using long iron runways. Will loved the wellhead so much he knew he had to possess it. After purchasing it, he had it shipped to San Francisco. It arrived several months later, eventually ending up as the center-piece attraction at his Pleasanton ranch, the ranch that had been owned by his father.

At age thirty, William had no money of his own. He was mortified having to ask his widowed mother for his $10,000 monthly allowance. He carried this resentment until the day she died. With Phoebe back home in Washington, D.C., his thoughts turned to his father's ranch in Pleasanton. He was looking for a place to escape and relax from his hectic life as a big-city newspaper editor. He envisioned transforming his father's hunting lodge into a luxurious country place where he could live life in a bachelor's paradise entertaining women and friends. In 1895, he hired respected San Francisco architect Albert Cicero Schweinfurth to modernize the old lodge. Schwein-furth determined that the house needed to be grand enough to display Will's growing art collection. His plan was to build it higher up the hillside on a gently sloping knoll above the fog and wind. Schweinfurth began to design the style with specialized rooms to assure privacy from visitors and servants. The house was constructed using balloon framing covered in white stucco. Balloon framing consisted of wood studs extending from the basement to the top of the home's three stories.

Schweinfurth intended the home to be, "A place, a man tired out with the cares and responsibilities of an active metropolitan life, could find absolute change where the feeling of *manana* could be cultivated." This is exactly what William was seeking, shelter from his fast-paced life. William named his new country home "El Rancho del Oso," which in Spanish means The Ranch of the Bears. He came up with this name while watching bear cubs at the 1894 California Mid-Winter International Exposition in Golden Gate Park. William bought the bears and had them transported by express wagon to his Pleasanton home. They were housed in a stockade built around an oak tree. The Verona wellhead was positioned in its place of honor in the center of the courtyard, and it was the first thing visitors saw upon entering through the entrance gates. It remained in that location until the 1920s when William had it shipped to his San Simeon ranch after his mother's death.

Described in the May 1896 issue of *American Architect,* Schweinfurth's original plan showed the structure to be a great square shape, 150 feet on each side, with a courtyard built around the Verona wellhead. Entrance to the hall was made through a *porte cochere* (covered patio). The dining room, library, and billiard room spanned the front while the other three sides were devoted to a bowling alley, seven guest

The courtyard before the Verona wellhead was placed.

apartments, and nine servant quarters. Family apartments were located in the two-story central block with two additional towers located nearby. The bathhouse was accessed by steps leading from the guest apartments. In simpler terms, the Hacienda had three sections connected by enclosed arbors, with the main center building having three stories. The south wing consisted of the guesthouse and music room. The north wing was the tank house and servant quarters.

William's dream of finishing his country home was shattered when his mother found out what he was doing at the property. Phoebe's friends in San Francisco had written letters to her in Washington, D.C., informing her what William was up to. Horrified, she raged to her niece Anne, "I will take the place … it's mine. He never said a word to me about building it." She was not going to allow him to take property, which legally belonged to her! She could not allow him to live there while throwing wild parties and putting the family reputation in jeopardy.

Downtrodden by this turn of events, William, age thirty-two, moved to New York City in 1895. At a crossroad in his life and career, he bought the struggling *New York Morning Journal,* eventually dropping *Morning* to become the *New York Journal.* With thoughts of Pleasanton still fresh in his mind, he vowed that someday, he would build his own hilltop mansion, and it would be grander than his mother's. His dream came true, and it's known today as Hearst's Castle, the glorious landmark

Carole MacRobert Steele

The Verona wellhead prominently displayed in the entrance courtyard accessed by the circular driveway. Courtesy of Pleasanton's Museum on Main.

that displays the family's art treasures and furnishings. Construction on the castle began in 1920, one year after his mother's death. Built on thousands of acres once owned by George Hearst, millions of tourists have visited this historical monument that opened to the public in 1958.

In 1896, Phoebe returned to California and took possession of the unfinished shell of a house. Schweinfurth stayed on as architect to finish construction. By 1897, the house was almost ready to occupy. Phoebe needed a telephone in the house, so she had a private phone line installed to insure her calls would not be delayed in transmission. Her phone number was FARMER 563. In 1900, while on a trip to Europe, Schweinfurth died from complications of typhoid fever, leaving the project uncompleted. Although the structure was unfinished, it was habitable, and Phoebe made the decision to move in.

Phoebe tended to be a hypochondriac, suffering from chronic illnesses with unexplained causes. Even a heart attack at age fifty-three didn't deter her from finishing construction on her home in Pleasanton. The doctor told her she'd survive, but that she needed to take better care of herself. This was all the more reason to make Pleasanton her permanent home. She could retreat to the Hacienda to relax and be free from the philanthropic and business activities that challenged her strength. She

348 — BIRDSEYE VIEW FROM UNIVERSITY OF CALIFORNIA, BERKELEY, CALIFORNIA.

EDWARD H. MITCHELL, PUBLISHER, SAN FRANCISCO.

1907 bird's eye view of the University of California at Berkeley. Phoebe was a highly respected regent and much-loved benefactress to this university.

was tired of people taking advantage of her generosity by making demands on her time and money.

She wasted no time in packing up her Washington, D.C., mansion, but she would keep it as a winter home until 1908. Using the unfinished plans of architect Schweinfurth, she was anxious to begin the arduous task of finishing her Hispano-Moresque style home. Schweinfurth referred to the design as Provincial Spanish Renaissance, but it was also described as California Mission style. For posterity, Phoebe wanted to document her home by hiring photographer Carleton Watkins. Since his eyesight had been failing since 1890, her home would be his last commission. He spent a year on the site, but was unable to complete the photography due to his inability to see clearly.

In 1903, after her son's hasty departure from the property, Phoebe invited newly established architect Julia Morgan to the Hacienda to discuss design changes that she wanted to make. Julia Hunt Morgan was born in 1872. By 1890, she was enrolled at the University of California at Berkeley. She planned to be a doctor, but her true interest was in the study of architecture. It was at the university where Phoebe and Julia would meet and begin a lifelong friendship. As a benefactress to the university for several years, Phoebe was heavily involved in campus activities. In 1897, she was the only woman, up to that time, to be appointed as a University of California regent. She loved young people (especially women), and enjoyed helping them pursue their

Carole MacRobert Steele

345 HEARST HALL, UNIVERSITY OF CALIFORNIA, BERKELEY

Funded by Phoebe in 1899, Hearst Hall at the University of California at Berkeley was named in honor of George Hearst. It burned down in 1922 in an accidental fire.

educational and career goals by offering scholarships, which became known as "Phoebes." The students and staff affectionately referred to her as their "fairy godmother." Phoebe had a house near the campus where she gave tea parties to entertain the young college women. It's possible that Julia met Phoebe while attending one of those parties; or they may have met when Julia participated in the International Architecture Competition, held for the purpose of choosing a person to design a new campus plan.

Phoebe had taken a great interest in Julia's ambitions and goals, and in 1894, Julia was the first woman at Berkeley to receive a degree in civil engineering, and the first woman in California to receive a license in architecture. One of Julia's male mentors at Berkeley encouraged her to attend the famous Ecole des Beaux-Arts (school of fine arts) in Paris, but it would take her three years to pass the entrance exam. Once enrolled in 1897, she soon became homesick and began writing letters to Phoebe expressing her loneliness. In response, Phoebe traveled to Paris and rented an apartment to be near Julia to encourage and support her. In 1902, and with Phoebe's help, Julia was the first woman from that school to earn a certificate in architecture. After graduation, Julia was back home in Oakland, California, where she opened her own architect business. Because of Phoebe's far-reaching influence and respect, she was able to make the contacts Julia needed in order to find employment in her chosen

Architect Julia Morgan (1872-1957). This photo, taken by her brother, shows her seated in the kitchen at the apartment they shared while she was a student at Ecole des Beaux-Arts School in Paris, France.

Carole MacRobert Steele

The Hacienda as seen in a photo postcard between 1907 and 1914.

The Hacienda as seen in a photo postcard between 1904 and 1918. An American flag can be seen on the flagpole. If the flag was raised, it indicated Mrs. Hearst was in residence.

field. Julia was part of the Berkeley campus design team responsible for planning the Hearst Mining Building in tribute to George Hearst. She was also hired to assist in the ongoing design and construction of the Hearst family German castle retreat known as Wyntoon, located on the McCloud River near Mt. Shasta, California. At a cost of $40,000, Wyntoon was started in 1902. Phoebe willed the property to her niece, Ann Apperson Flint. The Hearst family still owns it, but it's not open to the public.

Mrs. Hearst stopped all philanthropic activities to, "be free from the dozens of people who want things I cannot do." However, she stayed on as University regent

A guest of Phoebe's wrote on the front of this 1916 real photo postcard: "Veranda of Hacienda del Pozo de Verona –Mrs. Hearst's country house." The message written on backside: "We have just returned from another visit to Mrs. Hearst. These cards Mrs. Hearst had made for her friends and guests. You cannot buy postcards of her place. She might not permit the 'camera fiend' inside her gates. Says she does not want her home advertised that way. The beautiful porch is where 'tea' was served at 5 o'clock." Another publication describes the veranda as, "cool, with its massive beams and pillars and tiled flooring, provides a setting for tea."

until her death in 1919. Although the Hacienda had been completed by 1899, she wanted to devote more time to making design changes. Without hesitation, she hired Julia Morgan in 1903 to remodel, enlarge, and make the needed additions to the existing structure.

With sketch pad and pencil in hand, Julia knew this structure needed to be more than just a residence. It would have to be a home large enough to entertain family and friends, and to hold charitable functions—nothing but a mansion would do. The two women mutually agreed that the design should continue to be in the Spanish style that A. C. Schweinfurth had started.

While living in the carriage house at her parent's home in Oakland, Julia drew the house plans in extensive detail, adding several large rooms and extending the wide verandas. The roof line was multilevel with covered porches. Phoebe's house had the first indoor pool in California. The twenty by forty-foot pool was built into the ground with its entrance just one step down. The walls surrounding it were designed with

HEARST CASTLE - SAN SIMEON, CALIFORNIA

Not to be outdone by his mother, this 1950 postcard shows the main section of Hearst Castle in San Simeon, California. Overlooking the Pacific Ocean, this is the grand home William Hearst hired Julia Morgan to design. Julia made 558 train trips for weekend architectural sessions at the Castle. Her cost for construction was $4,717,000 and her architect's fee for the project was $70,755. She worked on the Castle from 1919 until 1942. William lived here until his death in 1951.

banks of glass doors. The roof and arched windows on three sides were also made of glass. Stands of flowers graced all the corners of the room. Phoebe kept forty-five to fifty bathing suits on hand at all times, insuring guests the use of the pool. A banquet room was added, as well as a forty by sixty-foot music room with ceilings thirty feet high. In addition, a ballroom, garage, carriage house, servant quarters, recreation buildings, and a stable with ten stalls were built on the estate, with Julia on hand for every detail of construction.

This dynamo of a young woman spent seven years of her life putting the final touches on Phoebe's dream home. A 1910 *Oakland Tribune* newspaper article said of the home: "Very beautiful additions have been made to the Hacienda under the direction of clever young architect Julia Morgan." As late as 1913, a new wing of the house was added, but Julia may not have been involved. She may have been too busy with other projects. Phoebe called her ninety-two-room mansion her "Hacienda," and it's here where her life on earth would come to an end. Julia's last correspondence with Phoebe was in March 1919. Word of Phoebe's death reached her while she was visiting Asilomar in Monterey County, another of the many buildings she designed. The woman who had been her mentor, benefactress, and friend was now gone, but the Hearst family was not done with Julia and her talents.

The same month his mother died, William Hearst moved back to California from New York. He wasted no time in approaching Julia about building his own dream home at San Simeon. One of his first thoughts was of his beloved Verona wellhead and having it as a centerpiece in his soon-to-be castle. Hearst Castle was probably Julia's greatest design achievement. With a career lasting forty-six years, Julia Morgan died February 2, 1957, at the age of eighty-five. She never married, and in her lifetime she designed 700 buildings that stand as her lasting legacy.

CHAPTER 2

HACIENDA DEL POZO DE VERONA

TRANSLATED, HACIENDA DEL POZO DE VERONA MEANS "THE HOUSE OF the Wellhead of Verona." A 1920s quote stated, "Mrs. Hearst was seeking to shelter the spirit of the Spanish dons when she built this Hacienda." Since its inception, the house had always been referred to as the "Hacienda." Other times it was referred to as "Verona Castle" after the celebrated wellhead William had brought over from Verona, Italy, in 1892.

The following is an excerpt written by Griswald North, taken directly from an article he wrote in 1900 for *The Puritan Magazine* titled "*A Summer Home in California.*" He stated that Phoebe lived there in the summers, while her winter home was in Washington, D.C:

> *In the great entrance hall, red and yellow are dominant in their native Spanish gaiety. Navajo blankets and serapes lend their lawless colorings, quaint Indian baskets stand for savagery, Spanish chests and rare old cabinets give suggestion of history. The most interesting room of all is the studio, a great raftered apartment seventy six feet long by forty three feet wide, which one enters by way of a colonnade lit by Spanish lamps. This has dressing rooms attached, and is often used for the overflow of a great house party, when all the bedrooms are full. The furniture, which came from Spain, is of old oak and includes a chest of Spanish leather and a seventeenth century German schrank; a receptacle for clothes and armor. Over the platform that crosses one end of the room is a very fine collection of armor.*

In 1904, an article appeared in *Country Life in America* naming the Hacienda as, "The greatest California patio house." It was also referred to as "The house of hospitality." One of her guests stated that it was, "A jewel of the kind that luxury, wealth and good taste can bring off only in such sumptuously endowed nature." The home was also cited as, "One of the most stately homes in California."

After taking a tour of the Hacienda in 1904, Barr Faree wrote an article titled

Taken from a 1900 issue of Puritan Magazine, *the caption reads: "The great raftered studio, seventy-six by forty feet, where the guests of the Hacienda are often assembled for entertainment." In reality, this is what Phoebe called the Music Room, the grandest room in her home. It was designed after an ancient monastery and decorated with art objects from all over the world. Adorning the room were tapestries, paintings, statues, busts, chests, vases, bowls, and cushions on the floor. On display, but not seen in this photo, was a piano and harp. This room could hold 300 people and was used for family weddings, christenings, and performances by famed musicians. A grand room for a grand lady, this was the appropriate place for Phoebe to lay in state upon her death.*

American Estates and Gardens, providing great descriptions of the house:

> *To the right as one enters are great apartments. To the left are servant quarters with a servant's hall in the corner. Both of these series of rooms are continued on the sides of the court, the guest rooms ending in a long bowling alley, the servants rooms being separated from the main building by a porch. The central structure by which one alights beneath a porte cochere [author's note: defined as a passageway through a building designed to let vehicles pass from the street to an interior courtyard, these were typical of eighteenth and nineteenth century mansions]. The main entrance includes a magnificent hall with a library and music room to the right and dining room to the left. The kitchen is beyond a passage opening out from the dining room. The corresponding space on the other side is filled by the billiard room. Splendidly furnished, fine works of art and household treasures and beamed ceilings.*

Many of the restful guest rooms opened directly onto picturesque patios. These patios were flanked on every side by building extensions, covered with multi-colored vines. This view shows the canopy-covered front door entrance accessed by the circular driveway with the Verona wellhead in the center. It is here where guests were dropped off upon their arrival to enter the home. Courtesy of Pleasanton's Museum on Main.

Phoebe furnished her home similar to the castles she'd visited in Europe. The Victorian Age was gaudy and elaborate, crowded with things of beauty. With that in mind, she supervised all the decorating, cramming her home with European art treasures, rare books, clocks, antique chests made of Spanish oak, Oriental rugs, and more. Tapestries hung high on the walls of the music room. Her collecting was impetuous and random. The interior had been described by a guest as, "the most original mixture of Greek, Roman, Medieval, Mexican, Chinese, Japanese, and Indian rarities." Her collection of paintings included nineteenth-century dark and traditional subjects mixed with portraits of European royalty. The rooms were adorned with antique lace, fans, enamels, miniatures, carved ivories, and other interesting curios. She adored sculpture and included several marble statues in her decorating scheme.

In 1897, while A. C. Schweinfurth was finishing up work on the house, Phoebe hired renowned botanist Luther Burbank to design and landscape the sizable estate

This ornate bronze Cellini gate opened into the State Dining Room. It had been in use for three centuries in a famous castle in Italy until Phoebe bought it on one of her European trips. Although it is said to have bore the date of 1642 and been the style of artist Benvenuto Cellini, it has not been proven to actually have been made by him.

Carole MacRobert Steele

The low ceiling living room (entrance hall), finished in mahogany, had as its centerpiece an onyx fireplace located in the center of the room near the front door. Hand-carved panels give a glimpse of the rare artistry to be found throughout the home in antique carved doors and rare old cabinets, precious old locks and hinge plates, and elaborate heavy draperies. Tapestries hang from the walls. Colorful reds and yellows found in Spanish designs helped to brighten the otherwise dark room. Strategically placed about the room are Navajo blankets, serapes and Indian blankets, all giving a flavor of the Spanish and California native influences. This room became the reception lobby for Castlewood Country Club.

grounds. When Burbank arrived, a road curving along the slope of the hills from the Verona railroad station was already in existence. On his first trip to the home, Burbank envisioned with great excitement the challenge of developing and enhancing the beauty of the existing landscape. With his botanical experience, knowledge, and talent, he knew with confidence, that he could accomplish this transformation. He was a kindly man, saying of himself, "I love flowers, trees, animals, and all works of nature." With an attitude like that, and his fine reputation, Phoebe felt assured that she had chosen the ideal person for the job. Known as California's "plant wizard," Luther lived his life as a botanist, horticulturalist, and a pioneer in agriculture science. He developed 800 strains and varieties of plants, fruits, flowers, grains, grasses, and vegetation, including his famous spineless cactus.

In 1914, an approaching visitor saw countless flowers and blooming shrubs growing profusely along the road, including many rare and beautiful exotics like the opulent rose-hued Japanese magnolia.

Throughout the years while Phoebe helped plan the landscaping, Burbank worked on enhancing the road leading to the Hacienda by lining it with exotic palms and half a dozen African date trees. Beneath the palms, he planted hedges of spineless cactus. On the sprawling lawns that were already in place, he planted varieties of oaks, dark conifers, madrones, evergreens, and fruit trees, many of which are alive and thriving today. By the turn of the century, Burbank had planted fifty acres of ornamental gardens. Where there had once been dirt, arriving guests now viewed endless beds of multi-colored flowers lining either side of the road, adding a rainbow of color among the palms and cactus.

Phoebe loved to host garden parties, accommodating up to 300 people at a time. Guests partied among the sights and scents of the plants that Burbank had chosen, which included: aralia, bamboo, banana trees, bird-of-paradise, camellia, cladium, ginger, longboats, magnolias, pomegranates, roses, tuberous begonia, tulip trees, white and pink lilies, and wisteria. Eighteen varieties of acacia trees graced the property and clementis clung to trellises. Japanese wisteria, hanging on lattice pergolas, cascaded from the stucco walls above. An arbor of grapes spanned the entire front of the house, and vines spread over the veranda walls. Multitudes of potted plants graced the corners of every patio. Ferns thrived in terra-cotta pots, and miniature

Carole MacRobert Steele

Luther Burbank's famous spineless cactus as seen in the Burbank Garden at his home in Santa Rosa, California. Burbank planted these in great abundance on the property, especially along the roadway leading to the Hacienda.

Tropical palm entrance drive landscaped by Luther Burbank.

A tranquil view showing miles of peaceful wooded hills afforded the Hacienda visitor to this privately owned old Spanish land grant.

palms swayed in the breeze. Behind the house lay three terraces laced with winding paths where visitors could stroll through a profusion of blooming flowers. Jasmine and roses, contained in earthenware pots, twisted up several thick pillars rising from the ground floor porch. Making their way along the exterior of the home, guests could leisurely saunter under trellised walkways. Pungent scents of perfumed vine blossoms filled the air along the "nun's walk."

In 1912, Phoebe was a member of the Luther Burbank Foundation, formed long after he completed the Hacienda project. He died in 1926, after an illustrious career spanning fifty-five years. He's buried near the greenhouse at his home in Santa Rosa, California, now a popular tourist attraction. In 1977, remnants of Burbank's plantings still remained. Pecan trees, an evergreen pear, weeping mulberries, and thornless Bankshire rose bushes still thrived on the property known as Castlewood Country Club. Also surviving through the decades was a bank of jasmine and a giant wisteria covering the stone wall of the old storage barn.

This was a working ranch as well as a home, and it needed to be self-sufficient. It was a mini-city unto its own. Functioning with modern plumbing and electricity, the estate had its own artisan well. The oil-fired boiler and steam engine, located in the pump house, forced the water uphill from the main reservoir to the auxiliary

Carole MacRobert Steele

The veranda of the fifty-three room main wing of the Hacienda in its eloquent solid comfort. This building contained treasures of art in ancient metalcraft, priceless hand-carved doors and walls, rare cabinets, and rich tapestries. Ornamental iron grilles covered the windows and little balconies opened to charming views of the countryside. All guest rooms had private or connecting baths. The foreground sloped to botanical gardens where graveled walks led to cozy nooks. Climbing vines and roses encircled the column architecture.

Vine-covered pillars and trellises along the Hacienda walkway.

Luther Burbank's fruitful spineless cactus as seen in 1908 at his home in Santa Rosa, California.

reservoir, supplying an unlimited amount of water. There was a two-ton ice plant, as well as machine and carpentry shops. Helping to keep the home cozy, sixty cords of firewood a year were needed for the fireplaces located throughout the expansive Hacienda. Another 11,000 gallons of fuel oil were consumed to keep the house warm. Phoebe encountered the household help every day, but she didn't speak with them directly; instead, her secretary passed on instructions for the day regarding the running of the house. The head housekeeper supervised a large staff of butlers, maids, and cooks. Employees were allowed to use the Verona station to catch a train into San Francisco to do their personal shopping. Thirty ranch hands maintained the 500 acres of land. Four stablemen and coachmen groomed, fed, and exercised twenty head of riding, buggy, and draft horses. The stable, built in 1896, was located an eighth of a mile from the main house. Phoebe didn't believe in washing machines; instead, ten women washed the laundry by hand. The expansive grounds surrounding the Hacienda were kept pristine by twenty-to-twenty-five gardeners who worked year-round to keep the foliage healthy and beautiful. No weeds, dry lawns, dead blooms, or untrimmed bushes would be tolerated.

By 1907, with the advent of the automobile, two chauffeurs were on standby at all times ready to transport Mrs. Hearst wherever she needed to go. A garage with a capacity to hold thirty-six cars was constructed. It housed three of her favorite lim-

Carole MacRobert Steele

"A great rambling structure sitting among ancient trees like an old patriarch and imposing its benevolent mood on all who pass. Like a corner of old Spain taking its ease away from the rushing centuries, the Hacienda is an elixir of content." These are words that have been used to describe the Hacienda as it's seen in this 1918 air view. A "station coach" can be seen parked at the front-door entrance in the circular driveway. This coach carried passengers from Phoebe's private Verona railroad station in Pleasanton to the Hacienda two miles away. The Verona wellhead is also visible in the courtyard.

ousines: a Pierce Arrow, Locomobile, and a Thomas Flyer. One of her higher-priced models was a twenty horsepower White Steamer, capable of carrying up to seven passengers. They were produced from 1901-1910. Automobiles were her preferred choice of transportation, ensuring a comfortable and quick ride to Verona station or to run errands in the little town of Pleasanton two miles down the hill.

People lucky enough to receive an invitation from the famed hostess began their trip aboard the Western Pacific, departing from Oakland, California. Travelers must have felt great excitement as they embarked on this one-and-a-half hour trek. Through the shallow hills of Niles Canyon (via Sunol), the tracks hugged the canyon walls along Alameda Creek. Cattle grazing on grassy slopes, or lying in the shade of a cottonwood tree, dotted the landscape. Startled by the roar and clamor of the train, deer lapping creek water bounded to safety to hide in the nearby brush. Soon the engine slowly chugged into view of the tiny but adequate Verona station. This little depot near Verona Road was built by Western Pacific especially for Mrs. Hearst to use as a

Railroad tracks and view looking up Niles Canyon. Scrub oak hills are what passengers saw on their train to Pleasanton.

Southern Pacific train crossing Alameda Creek in Niles Canyon. Pleasing vistas of hills and foliage along the route to and from Pleasanton.

Carole MacRobert Steele

Verona Station. This tiny, but adequate depot was designed by Julia Morgan for the private use of Phoebe Hearst and her guests. From here they arrived and departed by train. The design is in keeping with the same Spanish architecture as the Hacienda. Photo courtesy of the Bancroft Library, University of California, Berkeley.

"private shelter." Providing passengers protection from drenching rain or scorching sun, it was designed by Julia Morgan in the same Spanish style as the Hacienda. Tiles slanted down the roof of the rectangular-shaped stucco building. Above the heavy singular entrance door was the word VERONA in very large letters. Ornate iron accents adorned the white outer walls and the front door. When the train came to a stop, travelers stepped onto a wooden platform walkway. Depending on the weather, they might feel the warmth of the sun or the salty coolness of the air on their skin.

The sound of the tooting train whistle alerted Mrs. Hearst's coachmen or chauffeurs that the guests had arrived. Depending on the occasion or the size of the group, either automobiles, buggies, or carriages awaited the passengers. These conveyances transported them two miles up the dusty winding road through the low foothills of Pleasanton Ridge. Located on the third ridge above the County Road, the Hacienda was clearly visible from the valley floor. Its immense white towers stood out against a background of green-forested hills. Red Spanish tiles on the roof contrasted against a bright blue sky.

The dirt road guests traveled while riding in an automobile or horse and buggy. The Hacienda lay directly ahead in the low-lying hills. As this dirt road meandered through the valley, visitors passed through Phoebe's acres of orchards and fields of crops. Photo courtesy of Pleasanton's Museum on Main.

Backside of the Hacienda. From the balconies of their rooms, guests were able to enjoy the sight of the vast Livermore Valley below. These balconies in this three-story structure can be seen in this photo. Photo courtesy of Pleasanton's Museum on Main.

With orchards and arboretums on both sides, the route wound through 150 acres of bountiful apricot, cherry, fig, peach, and almond trees. Grapes and hops clung to vines, and every imaginable kind of vegetable was being grown, as well as corn, grain, and alfalfa to feed the livestock. Chickens, hogs, pheasants, ducks, and guinea hens were being raised to provide food. Twenty milk cows provided dairy products. The road meandered past the stables where twenty draft and riding horses were sheltered. All this bounty was sustained to feed members of the household as well as guests. The town was very amiable towards Mrs. Hearst, because whatever wasn't grown on the ranch was obtained from the merchants in Pleasanton. Phoebe loved to watch her gardens grow in the abundant rich soil. She delighted in picking fragrant flowers that grew near the house, and she could claim one of the largest tulip gardens on the entire coast. In the glass-enclosed conservatory, and under ideal conditions, a large collection of rare flowers bloomed profusely. On a daily basis, the scent of freshly cut blossoms filled the air in the Hacienda. When gala events were held, vases and urns of flowers enhanced the ambiance of the rooms. Nothing pleased Phoebe more than to see the look of surprise on the faces of her guests as she presented them with fresh strawberries, sweet cherries, or fuzzy peaches to take home and enjoy. If they were really lucky, a colorful box of blossoms was given as a parting gift.

On the ride up the hill, visitors may have noticed members of the native Ohlone tribe sitting by the side of the road. Members of this tribe were allowed to have a small village on the estate. Phoebe helped many of the Ohlone women by hiring them to work in the Hacienda's steam laundry, located a distance from the main house.

As the journey continued up the road, the majestic Hacienda came into full view. The lane flattened out, becoming straight and dignified and befitting the entrance to a mansion of such magnitude. Travelers saw before them a creamy-white stucco building of Spanish-Moorish design. The central section, three stories high, was surrounded by smaller towers. This was not an ornate edifice; instead, it loomed like a cement fortress exuding wealth and refinement. The lady behind its walls was indeed a person of wealth and refinement. Lush green lawns surrounded the home, while a variety of ornamental plants and shrubbery flanked its textured walls. Ferns in huge earthenware pots stood at intervals along the upper parapets. The Hacienda, 750 feet in length, had corridors going east and west, each containing functional rooms and guest apartments. The upper-story windows were shaded by colorful striped awnings. Decorative wrought iron grilles covered these windows, adding character to otherwise plain glass. Some of the rear windows had little balconies where guests could view Mt. Diablo to the north, breaking the Livermore Valley skyline. If their room was in the front of the Hacienda, guests could look upon green-forested hills

Known as the Verona Bridge, this truss across the Arroyo de la Laguna is located between Pleasanton-Sunol Road and Foothill Road was built to carry guests to the Hacienda. This pleasant arroyo stream running through the property was more like a lagoon when the Hearsts bought the property.

Carole MacRobert Steele

Looking toward the hills from the main building of the Hacienda. Palm trees line the road as it enters the causeway to the entrance gates in the foreground.

and vast expanses of lawns, trees, and gardens.

At the entrance to the courtyard stood two Medieval-looking guard towers. Hanging between these towers was a Moorish-style ornamental iron gate held in place by decorative hinges. There were no actual guards posted at the towers, but the gate stayed opened during the day. At nightfall, in keeping with Spanish tradition, the gate was closed by the grounds man. If Mrs. Hearst was in residence, a flag waved from its pole to indicate that she was home. It was through these conical-shaped towers that guests entered the courtyard to behold its most prominent object, the magnificent Verona wellhead for which the Hacienda was named. Invited guests stepped out of the carriage under the covered overhang. The massive carved front door opened slowly as Phoebe greeted her guests. Standing with the grand entrance hall directly behind her, she extended her warm, but now wrinkled, hand to welcome them. With twinkling eyes and a subdued smile, she might have given them a hug if they were family, otherwise just a handshake.

Although tired from the train ride, the visitors senses are heightened by what they see. Even before they are offered refreshments or shown to their rooms, Mrs. Hearst

A first glimpse of the magnificent Hacienda that greeted guests and visitors as they crossed the causeway.

is anxious and proud to show them the grandeur of her home. As their ultimate tour guide, she leads the way from room to room, her taffeta gown rustling along the bare floors. Trying to take it all in, the new arrivals begin to feel like they're in a museum of antiquities. With the tour of the house over, they're ready to rest and settle in for an overnight stay. Every modern convenience awaits them. A butler or maid appears to show them to their rooms located on the second story. Once in the room, they might sit in one of the side chairs positioned in the plushly furnished room; or they may step over to the window to take in the breathtaking view of the valley or the hills. A relaxing sip of sherry would taste good, but Phoebe politely asks that no liquor be consumed in the room. With the ring of a bell, they were able to summon a maid to draw the bath. Stepping into the mammoth marble tub, the comforting warm water slowly eases away the happy stress of the day. Though totally relaxed while soaking, the jingling of the phone in the room may be startling. It might be an anxious friend calling to hear the details of the trip to Mrs. Hearst's Hacienda.

Depending on who you are and what you're there for, Phoebe has already planned and organized the activities in advance. Whatever the event, it will be on a grand scale and never to be forgotten. The occasion will be lavish, the food divine, the surroundings awe-inspiring, and, above all, enjoyable. If the guests feel like they've been entertained like royalty in a castle, the hostess has accomplished her goal! Feeling a little hungry on the train ride back to Oakland, the traveler might want to snack on succulent strawberries picked fresh from Phoebe's own garden. She happily sent these along with her guests as a pleasant reminder of a most enjoyable visit.

A woman of great contradiction, Phoebe loved having company and giving par-

The Hacienda front door with the Verona wellhead plainly in view. Striped window awnings and terra cotta pots add color to an upper patio. Photo courtesy of Pleasanton's Museum on Main.

Flagpole with the American flag waving.

Portly medieval towers guarded the massive iron-studded entrance doors that opened up into the entrance courtyard. It was the duty of the guardsman to close these gates each night.

ties, but she cherished her privacy. When she entertained, her invitees ranged from university students to performers of the arts, royalty, and even President McKinley and President Taft. As hostess, Phoebe enjoyed making a grand entrance from the gallery staircase. Perhaps dressed in a lavender gown made of satin brocade, she descended the steps to her waiting guests in the dining room below, its walls covered in garnet-colored velvet. When dinner was called, Phoebe took her appointed seat at the center of the long elegant table, which accommodated up to forty-two people. A typical weekend party often consisted of dozens of people who were offered full use of the house, pool, and the entire property—to roam about as they pleased. Phoebe preferred to meet and socialize with her guests one hour before dinner. She felt her time was valuable and the hours after dinner could be better spent working on business affairs in the comfort of her bedroom suite.

Having 300 people for a garden party or wedding was common, and she could easily accommodate fifty for an outdoor dinner. Every spring she invited the university's senior class from Berkeley to come to the Hacienda for an afternoon picnic. Such was the case in 1902, when a special train pulling five passenger cars brought 300 graduating seniors. They left Oakland at 11 o'clock, arriving at Verona station

Carole MacRobert Steele

State Dining Room where kings and queens and great artists have been entertained.

The State Dining room measured sixty by thirty feet and was also called the Cellini room. It was through this ornate bronze gate, supposedly carved by Italian artist Benvenuto Cellini, that distinguished guests arrived for formal dinners. Designed in early Spanish style, the room had huge windows that looked out on the valley. These windows were framed by silk tapestry drapes. The walls were covered in red velvet and the floors made of highly polished hardwood. Food was served from a massive buffet of carved wood, and the dining table and chairs were made of carved mahogany.

an hour-and-a-half later. Dozens of horse-drawn surreys were ready and waiting to take them to the Hacienda. Mrs. Hearst greeted them in a room located off the main hall, where she promptly escorted them to the art gallery. Viewing the treasures in this collection was a way to keep the students entertained until luncheon was served.

Mrs. Hearst mingled freely among the young people, pleasantly chatting with as many of them as she could. She may have asked about their future plans or about their classes and activities at the University. When lunch was announced, the students made their way to tables set up on the porches and verandas. Tents were also pitched on the lawns to accommodate more seating. The proportions of food were so large that it seemed more like a dinner meal than a lunch. When the luncheon was over, Yanke's Orchestra provided music for an impromptu dance under the crimson and gold awning that spanned the porch roof. Other students were eager to explore the nearby stables to see the horses and extravagant tack equipment. In 1959, these stables and a nearby two-story building were destroyed by fire. The buildings stabled not only the horses, but also served as living quarters for the coachmen and servants.

Phoebe posing in one of her Hacienda courtyards, appearing the way she may have looked as she bid her guests farewell. Photo courtesy of Pleasanton's Museum on Main.

　　　　Carole MacRobert Steele

The fire burned for two hours, destroying valuable farm equipment, and scorching several ancient oak trees. The fun events of the day passed all too quickly for the merry throng who were still curious to explore more of the estate. Sadly, their time for departure had arrived. At 4:30, the carriages arrived promptly to transport them to Verona station and the special train waiting to take them back to the Bay Area. The students yelled cheers to a smiling Mrs. Hearst as she waved good-bye to them from her front door.

In 1903, Phoebe was thrilled at the prospect of hosting the wedding of her niece, Anne Apperson. An *Oakland Tribune* article described the event:

> *For days carpenters constructed in the music room, an altar six feet wide. Candles in antique brass candelabras and vases filled with white tiger lilies. Behind the altar was a large painting of the Holy Family. Suspended from the rafters were asparagus ferns. Great baskets of pink and white flowers. Garlands on every cabinet and tall vases of ferns. Palms and tropical foliage on either side of the room. All the flowers, including those for the bride, came from the Hacienda conservatory. A tent-like canopy covered the outdoor courtyard for the breakfast served after the wedding.*

Having multitudes of costumes to choose from, Phoebe loved to host and participate in masquerade balls at her home, a tradition she started while in Washington, D.C., when she hosted her first ball. Dozens of trunks filled with all types of costumes were stored in a concrete warehouse at the rear of the Hacienda. This building also served as a depository for the overflow of antiques and art that she had stockpiled. The party-goers had their choice of elaborate clothing to present themselves as kings, queens, knights, or court jesters. Attendees could also opt to wear native attire from Egypt, Persia, China, Japan, Mexico, Sweden, or France. Matching shoes, wigs, jewelry, and hats were available to help authenticate the ensemble.

Exhausted after any party, Phoebe often retired to her private apartment above the music room, where she was comfortably surrounded by all the things she loved: her tapestries, paintings, Oriental rugs, rare clocks, native artifacts, bronzes, and more. Although weary from the evening's festivities, she was known to work at her desk well in the middle of the night going over finances or planning another party! She often laid in bed reading a good book, with cushioned pillows propped behind her back for added support. While in bed and snuggled in a warm satin bed jacket, she used a table tray across her lap to write letters until her weary eyes begged to close for the night. An ordinary day was never dull in the life of Phoebe Apperson Hearst.

Phoebe as she looked in 1912 wearing her customary ostrich-plumed bonnet, lace clothing, a strand of pearls tight at the neck, and curls at her forehead. In photos, she's often seen wearing these pearls. They obviously had sentimental value to her.

CHAPTER 3

THE TURN OF THE CENTURY AND THE END OF AN ERA

PHOEBE DIVIDED HER TIME BETWEEN THE HOME SHE STILL OWNED IN Washington, D.C., and the Hacienda in Pleasanton. The population of Pleasanton in the 1900 census was 1,500, but Phoebe was not among the populace. She was listed as residing in a six-room apartment in San Francisco, and with her in that apartment were two housemaids and a cook. When Phoebe was questioned by the census worker, she reported her occupation as capitalist. A capitalist is defined as: "A person who profits in accordance with the principles of Capitalism, and Capitalism is defined as an economic system in which investment and ownership and the exchange of wealth is made and maintained chiefly by private individuals." This definition described her status perfectly.

While Phoebe was moving in and decorating her Hacienda, William, age 30, was still a bachelor, but he was not lonely. Much to his mother's dismay, he continued to be fascinated with showgirls. He regularly attended vaudeville acts, flirting shamelessly with the girls backstage. As early as 1897, Millicent Wilson, a sixteen-year-old chorus girl, caught his eye. Around this time, he also met a pretty young actress named Marion Davies. As with Millicent, he was quite a bit older than Marion. Though he never married Marion, he played a big part in promoting her movie career, and she ended up being the woman he'd spend the majority of his life with.

Totally smitten with Millicent, William courted her for six years before they married in 1903. She was twenty-two and he was forty. Phoebe couldn't bear the thought of him marrying a girl in show business, so she shunned the wedding using illness as an excuse to stay away. In lieu of attending, she sent the happy couple a congratulatory telegram. William would have preferred that his mother be at the wedding, feeling happy that at long last he'd found someone to love. The ceremony took place at Grace Episcopal Church in Manhattan, witnessed by a group of the couple's closest friends. Several weeks passed before the newlyweds arrived at the Hacienda for a visit, at which time Phoebe presented the bride with a stunning emerald brooch as a wedding gift.

Phoebe looking very proud holding her first-born grandchild, George Randolph Hearst, affectionately called "Buster." He was born 1904 and died in 1972, having reached the level of vice-president of the Hearst Corporation. Courtesy of Library of Congress LC-DIG-ggbain-04990.

Carole MacRobert Steele

Phoebe in a 1917 photo with her five grandsons in the Hacienda entrance courtyard. These are the children of William Randolph Hearst and his wife, Millicent: William Randolph Jr., twins Elbert David and Randolph Apperson, George Randolph, and John Randolph. No girls were ever born to the family. Photo courtesy of Pleasanton's Museum on Main.

In 1904, the first of their five children was born five days before their first wedding anniversary. The baby was named George "Buster" Randolph Hearst. With each of the following births, Phoebe hoped with all her heart for a little girl, but it was never to be. William Randolph Jr. was born in 1908, followed by John Randolph in 1910, and twins Randolph Apperson and David Whitmire in 1915. Throughout their lives, the boys called their dad "Pop." Phoebe never entirely accepted Millicent, but she eventually warmed up to her with the realization that she'd given her five adorable grandsons whom she dearly loved. Millicent and the boys lived with Phoebe at the Hacienda every summer and for other extended periods of time. Grandma Phoebe wished they could be around more often so she could have an influence on their lives; just as she'd had on Will's life. She spoiled them just as she'd spoiled Will. Her wish for the boys was that they lead a simple and natural child's life. Since she was giving William $10,000 a month for the support of his sons, he had no objection to them spending more time with their grandmother. He wanted his sons to grow up in California, not living in New York City.

Christmas at the Hacienda was filled with the joyous sounds of five rambunctious boys. It must have been music to Phoebe's ears to hear their happy squealing when she played hide-and-seek with them in the magical music room. There were endless nooks and crannies where she could hide, waiting in anticipation of them finding her. In the center of this opulent room stood the freshly cut fir tree, its pine aroma filling the air. Dozens of shiny ornaments hung on its branches as they glittered in the flicker of lit candles. Beneath the tree lay gaily wrapped packages containing several toys for each boy. Among the gifts, most certainly, were books to stimulate their young minds. No doubt the five cherub-cheeked boys eagerly waited to open the hand-picked presents given to them by their doting grandmother.

Phoebe loved shopping and buying gifts for family, friends, and employees. She started shopping in January, and she shopped all year until the following Christmas; however, most Christmas gifts had been purchased by mid-summer. On December first, her staff began cataloging, wrapping, and addressing packages at a table in the "Christmas Room" (music room). Phoebe was on hand to supply the names of all the people on her gift list, and records were kept to make sure that no one got the same gift twice. In a timely manner, all packages were inscribed, addressed, and readied for dispatch to lucky recipients. Thousands of gifts were stacked and stored on shelves and drawers in the Christmas Room, ready to be packaged and mailed.

Seated in a velvet-covered chair, Phoebe must have watched with delight as each lad excitedly ripped into his package, anxious to discover its contents. Toward afternoon, when most of the excitement had died down, aromas emanated from the kitchen with the promise of a sumptuous dinner. On the ornately carved dining room table, draped in lace or white linen, were elegant place settings of fine china, polished silverware, gleaming glassware, and starched napkins. From her place of honor at the center of the table, Phoebe could easily see and converse with her family members. When everyone was seated, uniformed servants arrived from the kitchen carrying silver trays of assorted holiday food. The entree was either turkey, goose, or ham—or all three! For dessert, the adults might have savored rich plum pudding while the children munched on brightly decorated cookies and gingerbread men. Phoebe must have felt blessed taking in the sights and sounds of this wonderful day, but more than likely, she couldn't help but wish George were there to enjoy it with her. She probably felt great sadness knowing that he never lived long enough to see his first grandchild born. Her heart surely warmed as she gazed at her beloved son, William, seated at the head of the table. Most certainly he was proud of his five handsome sons seated beside him, feeling confident that their existence was the one thing that brought pride and happiness to his mother.

Carole MacRobert Steele

Mrs. Phoebe Apperson Hearst

Dated 1918, this photo shows an always elegant and refined Phoebe. She holds an ornate fan in her lap, no doubt bought on one of her worldwide trips. She must not have changed hairstyles over the years, because the curls at her forehead show in most photos of her.

Casa Bonita, translated in Spanish, means beautiful house, but Phoebe called it the Boys' House. The Spanish style two-story structure was built solely to house her five grandsons when they stayed with her for extended periods of time. It was built near the main house in a grove of oak trees. Salmon in color, it was built in 1909 or 1910 when Phoebe realized she needed a place where the boys could be well attended by nannies and surrounded by every imaginable convenience and toy a boy could want. After being abandoned and vandalized for several years, it was torn down in 1982 and turned into a parking lot. Photo courtesy of Pleasanton's Museum on Main.

With the arrival of William's third son, Phoebe decided that an additional house needed to be built on the property to accommodate all of them. The same Spanish style would be used, and Julia Morgan was her first choice as architect. A site was chosen close to the main house near a grove of oak trees. The "Boys' House," as Phoebe called it, was also known as Casa Bonita, meaning "beautiful house" in Spanish. When completed, the Boys' House had two stories and was painted pink. It consisted of thirteen rooms, including three bedrooms on either side and two at each end. Each boy had his own room. Nothing but the best for the boys; just as it had been for boy-child William. Tutors, nurses, and governesses were hired to care for them, and each was provided with his or her own living quarters, enabling him or her to be in close proximity to the boys twenty-four hours a day.

Books to entertain and educate filled the multitude of shelves in the library. Pictures were hung to add color and eye-appeal to otherwise drab walls. The schoolroom and living room were downstairs. Since Phoebe spent a great deal of time in toy stores, the downstairs playroom contained every toy imaginable, including a miniature railroad. The downstairs was so large, the toddlers had enough room to ride their tricycles up and down the hall. In the gym, they could work off some of their abundant energy. The garden provided an area for the boys to play games, make castles in the giant sandbox, swing high on the swings, and pedal kiddie cars on cobbled pathways. The boys surely got a kick out of being pulled around the yard by dogs hooked up to a cart. This was a popular trend during this time period and they were called "dog carts." Play suits hung neatly in the closets, allowing the governesses to make sure each boy had a clean change of clothes for meals and school time. Phoebe grew up riding horses, so she was able to help teach the boys how to ride their ponies. Their favorite pony was named "Brownie." As adults, all the boys became skilled horsemen, an ability grandpa George would have been proud of. She surely derived much joy knowing how deeply they loved her. Their childhood, spent at Casa Bonita, provided them with a lifetime of happy memories. In many ways, William had been a disappointment to his mother, but he'd given her the gift of these wonderful children that kept her feeling young in the latter years of her life. Casa Bonita was destined to have its own interesting, but uncertain future, and that was a future that Phoebe would not live to see.

The 1910 census shows sixty-seven year old Phoebe still residing in Pleasanton. She's listed as Mrs. P. A. Hearst living on a private estate, making her own income. Her household members are listed as: butler, carpenter, chamber boy, chauffeurs, coachmen, cooks, dressmaker, electrician, engineer, gardeners, housekeeper, laborers, ladies maid, laundress, maid, and nurse. The oldest worker is a seventy-year-old man, and the youngest is a twenty-year-old man. Most of the employees were single and Caucasian, but there were also English-speaking Chinese, Italians, and Germans. Grandsons George, age six, and William, age two and one-half, were also listed as living with her. By 1917, her health was beginning to fail. Her slight body, weakened by age, no longer had the strength to make it up the long flight of stairs to her bedroom suite. Fred McCormac, her longtime trusted Hacienda manager, carried Phoebe like a child in his arms up the steps to her bedroom. The beauty of her youth had faded, her pale brown hair now silvered with gray, her lips thin and colorless, and her cheeks lacking any hint of rosiness.

In December 1918, Phoebe was in New York City visiting William, Millicent, and her grandsons. By January, the cold she'd been suffering from worsened. She was diagnosed with the dreaded Spanish Flu. This epidemic (1918-1919), was running rampant through San Francisco and killing millions of people worldwide, but she insisted on returning to California. She left New York City, taking with her grandsons William Jr. and John, along with several friends. Traveling on a special train back to the

A view of Main Street in Pleasanton in the 1907-1915 era showing a candy parlor and millinery shop. The enclosed buggy seen on the right is the type Mrs. Hearst may have used to run errands to Pleasanton, which was located two miles down the hill from the Hacienda.

West Coast, she was accompanied by only the best nurses and most qualified doctors.

There was speculation she may have contracted the flu from one of her servants who had been in San Francisco visiting or shopping. Once home, she felt cheery and enlightened to be in her own surroundings. With three doctors in attendance, including her own physician Dr. Ray Lyman Wilbur, her condition seemed to improve, but within a few days she became gravely ill. William was telegraphed immediately of her critical condition. With great haste and time of the essence, he and Millicent left New York City to travel to California. Phoebe rallied her first week home, but at 4:15 Easter morning, April 13, 1919, the grand lady died in her sleep from complications of pneumonia. The son she adored, even with his faults, was at her bedside. Her frail hand resting in his, she took her last breath. Now with her hand stilled, entries in her diaries would come to an end, and her large gray eyes closed for the last time. Hacienda del Pozo de Verona would never be the same.

"The Empress," as she was referred to by Washington, D.C., elite, passed quietly, but perhaps not peacefully. She'd still had so much to see and do, trips to take, grandsons to watch grow, and a son to see become famous and infamous. She passed away surrounded by the cherished possessions she loved. She was remembered as, "The giver, loving friend, devoted mother, and wise counselor." Phoebe's twin grandsons

Mrs. Hearst's bedroom at the Hacienda. In this bed, she died from complications of the flu in 1919. Several family photos are prominent on the walls, including one that looks like her husband George. A large madonna and child painting hangs above the bed. The room is furnished typically the way the rest of the house was … like a museum. In her bedroom, she was comforted and surrounded by personal things that meant the most to her. Courtesy of Library of Congress LC-USZ62-54536.

were only four when she died and hardly old enough to have truly known her. Fifteen-year-old George, the oldest, would surely remember his days spent in Pleasanton under the watchful eye of his grandmother.

Phoebe Hearst packed an enormous amount of life into her seventy-seven years. She was a complicated woman of extreme contradictions. She was frugal, but spent lavishly. She was in poor health, but had enough energy to travel the world. She loved company and entertaining, but valued her privacy. She was shy and hated publicity, but she exuded an air of aristocracy. She hated politics, but was married to a senator. As a middle-aged woman, Phoebe had thrived on challenges and dealing with crises, but in her elderly years she commented that, "Life had gotten richer and sweeter." Her goal had not been to gain celebrity, but to undertake civil responsibilities. She wanted to be remembered by her creed: "Community service and a wish for people to be on time, have good manners, and respect older people." Some final words spoken in tribute to her character referred to her as: "A gentle woman and public servant, a blessing to her day and generation."

Clothed in her favorite lavender gown, she lay in a satin-lined casket. The casket was placed in the center of the magnificent music room, surrounded by multitudes of her favorite flowers. She was finally at peace. The plans she had been making for a trip to the Orient would have to wait for perhaps another lifetime. Friends and family attended the private gathering in the music room. Another service was held at Grace Episcopal Church in San Francisco as federal flags were lowered in observance of her death, and dignitaries from all over California arrived to pay their respect. Hundreds of University of California Berkeley students, attired in cap and gown, were also there to honor her. While the eulogy was being performed, a public memorial was also held at the civic auditorium. The organ played while three vested choirs sang songs she loved. One of the choirs accompanied the entourage to the Hearst family mausoleum at Cypress Lawn Cemetery in Colma, California, where she was interred next to her husband. Pallbearers included the mayor of San Francisco and California Governor William D. Stephens.

Mrs. Hearst left a twenty-two-page will that was written in 1911, but in 1917 and 1918, she added two codicils. With reference to the Hacienda, she stated, "No one will live there after I'm gone." It was her intention that William not inherit it. She left instructions for the estate to be sold with the proceeds going to her five grandsons. Their inheritance also included the Hearst Building in San Francisco, and other real estate holdings. William made his feelings clear about the Hacienda stating that, "It was pleasant, but didn't offer the escape that San Simeon did." The ranch at San Simeon was left to William, and with that, he never looked back. He had a castle to build!

Her estate was estimated between five and ten million dollars, with bequests to family members ranging from $25,000 to $250,000. Her niece, Anne Apperson Flint, received $250,000 and the Wyntoon retreat at Mt. Shasta. Elbert, Phoebe's brother was given $150,000. Servants and friends were bequeathed between $1,000 and $5,000. The University at Berkeley was a main beneficiary, receiving $60,000 for scholarship funds, as well as several art objects, rugs, tapestries, paintings, sculptures, and more. Phoebe left to William: "All the rest, residue and remainder of my estate, real, personal, or mixed and whatsoever situated I give, desire and bequeath unto my beloved son William Randolph Hearst." As her only child, the family portraits and heirlooms also went to him to be passed on to future generations of Hearsts. It also fell on him to disburse the contents of the Hacienda, which contained hundreds of

Phoebe Hearst as she looked in 1912, seven years before she died. Still wearing furs, lace, and fancy hats, her beauty long since faded.

items they had purchased together on their early trips to Europe. To understand her will is to understand the events leading up to the writing of it. William continued his affair with Marion Davies while he was still married to Millicent. Phoebe was so angry and disturbed by this, she changed her will, leaving the Hacienda to her five grandsons. Clever man that he was, Will interceded his son's inheritance with legal maneuvering, and obtained the rights to the Hacienda. Although as late as 1921, Will and the boys still visited the Hacienda to celebrate such things as the Fourth of July. By 1924, he sold the home and 500 acres to a group of Bay Area businessmen who intended to turn the property into a prestigious country club. His sons loved the Hacienda and protested it being sold to strangers, but their hands were tied. The year of the sale, seventeen expert packers loaded up carloads of furnishings to be dispersed to Wyntoon and the castle at San Simeon.

When news of the affair with Marion Davies became public in 1926, William and Millicent became estranged. He wanted a divorce, but she would never grant him one. They remained married, but led separate lives. She lived in New York City, leading the life of a socialite, while he lived in San Simon with Marion as his mistress and constant companion. At the time of his death in 1951, it was reported that William left Marion fifty-one percent of his fortune.

Phoebe had not been shy about letting her son know that she wanted to be honored and remembered with some type of memorial after her death. One month after she died, William talked with Julia Morgan about his plans for the ranch property in San Simeon. As early as 1905, he had approached her about taking on his immense building project. His true motivations may never be known for building San Simeon in the magnitude that he did, but it was speculated that he built it to honor his mother—or despite his mother!

Even with his shortcomings, San Simeon could be considered a monument to William's own success. He'd made his own fortune without his mother's help. No longer would he have to ask for handouts as he'd done for most of his fifty-six years. If she had artifacts and art, he had more! If she had a mansion, he had a castle!

In his San Simeon castle, he honored his mother by displaying the art, furniture, and artifacts that had been removed from the Hacienda after her death. Although he was the one who bought the Verona wellhead, it had remained in the Hacienda courtyard the entire time Phoebe lived there. He could not leave it behind; it needed to be removed and relocated to San Simeon. Ninety-four years later, the pink wellhead still sits in a stately place of honor on the South Earring Terrace near cottage A at San Simeon State Park, a historical monument visited yearly by millions of tourists. A photo of George Hearst hung in Phoebe's bedroom at the Hacienda. That same photo can be seen hanging on the wall in William's master bedroom suite at Hearst Castle. At the main entrance to Hearst's Castle is a small obscure plaque that reads: "La Cuesta Encantanda," a present to the State of California in 1958 by the Hearst Corporation in memory of William Randolph Hearst, who created this Enchanted Hill, and of his Mother, Phoebe Apperson Hearst, who inspired it."

Although she collected foreign art and furnished her homes with European antiques, Phoebe cherished most of all, the personal items that had a special meaning; items representing home, affection, and family. When it was time for William to move, distribute, and sell her belongings, he discovered a two-story forty-by-one hundred-foot warehouse on the Hacienda property. Stored inside the building were collections of books, paintings, prints, antique furniture, marble statues, bronzes, porcelain, a silver-mounted Mexican saddle, and more. It turns out his mother was a pack rat. Two trunks of paper brimmed with: faded, musty, and outdated telegrams, yellowing newspaper clippings, greeting cards, paid bill stubs, shopping tags, sales lists of commodities and collections, notices of meetings, social invitations, and more. Items deemed worthless were discarded and burned. The Hacienda would not lay dormant for long. Only a few short years would pass before it would experience a rebirth.

CHAPTER 4

A COUNTRY CLUB IS BORN

THOMAS W. NORRIS, PRESIDENT OF CASTLEWOOD COUNTRY CLUB FROM 1925 to 1929, believed that: "A country club should provide different sports for members. Everyone doesn't play golf, ride, or swim, but nearly everyone plays something. The play of many sports will be available at Castlewood, combined with unusually attractive social activities and country life." According to heraldic standards, the Club's crest colors of black and gold embodied the name of the Club and its activities. Over the years, there have been rumors and speculation about how Castlewood got its name. Phoebe Hearst's Hacienda, located 516 feet above sea level, was surrounded by wooded hills. From the valley, her house looked like a castle with its white walls and towers. Therefore, people referred to it as "the castle on the hill," or "castle in the woods." Shortened to Castlewood, this name appealed to the owners so much, they decided to incorporate the Club under that title. It remained Castlewood until 1940 when it was renamed Old Hearst Ranch under new ownership.

We can only guess how Phoebe would have felt about her home being turned into a country club. Knowing her home and land would be enjoyed by wealthy families, she probably would have approved. She could rest in peace knowing her estate would continue to be well-cared for. Her home had always been open to invited guests, and now a group of prominent Bay Area businessmen were inviting prosperous men and their families to join the newly established Castlewood Country Club—for a price! One of the goals of the new owners was to save the estate from sub-dividers. The buildings and acreage had an appraised value of $1.5 million dollars. President Norris stated they had acquired the property for a ridiculously low price with no encumbrances, except an issue of bonds owned by the Club members. They envisioned building a golf course that would rival none. Because of its location on the sheltered eastern slope of the Coast Range Mountains, the Club was in the "sunshine belt" and out of the fog. There was sunshine all day, and the scenic beauty and sportiness was comparable to any in the world. The owners hope was to create a sportsman's Elysium and to preserve all the charm that embodied California's finest tradition of hospitality. They planned to keep everything the same, using all the same facilities

Carole MacRobert Steele

This embossed logo image appears on the cover of the Castlewood Country Club promotional booklet produced in 1926. The booklet measures ten inches by thirteen inches and contains thirty photos, several of which appear in this book. The symbols inside the logo indicate what Castlewood Country Club represented.

This postcard postmarked 1931 shows the lush foliage planted by Luther Burbank on the winding lane leading to Castlewood Country Club.

1930s view of the three-story clubhouse with the road in the foreground showing how much the trees and foliage had matured since being planted thirty years prior.

Carole MacRobert Steele

1920s postcard captioned on front: Looking down the driveway, Castlewood Country Club. This shot was taken under the vine-covered arch between the two guard towers looking toward the hills. On the left side of the road was the proposed golf fairway showing the natural beauty and character of the terrain.

Photo postcard postmarked 1930. Taken directly from the 1926 Club booklet: "La Hacienda del Pozo de Verona, acquired for an incredibly low figure, is probably the most fortunate investment ever made by a country club; not only because of the actual value represented by its buildings, picturesque territory, and water rights, but because it has a rare felicity of character that is beyond price." This image shows golfers on the right and tennis courts on the left. The tennis courts would eventually be the site of the new swimming pool. American flag waves from the flagpole.

1930s photo postcard shows entrance gates to the Clubhouse. A small sign posted says: To the Locker Room, Professionals Shop and Caddie House. An arrow on the other sign points to the driveway down between the palms.

Phoebe had utilized. The only exception was that a portion of the acreage was going to be transformed into a golf course. With dignitaries in attendance and several events planned, it was an all-day celebration when the Club officially opened in April 1926.

Castlewood's membership office was located in the Richfield Oil building in San Francisco. In 1926, from these offices, the Executive Committee mailed ten-inch by thirteen-inch elegantly printed and bound booklets to prospective members. The embossed black and gold Castlewood crest graced the front cover. Each booklet contained forty-two pages, including thirty black and white photos showing the buildings and grounds. One of the photos was an air view looking down on the entire property. The title page read: Former Estate of Mrs. Phoebe A. Hearst. On the last page was a layout drawing of the proposed golf course designed by famous course architect William "Billy" Bell. The Board of Directors and officers were listed, naming Thomas W. Norris as president. Norris wrote the booklet's foreword with his occupation listed as president of the Coast Manufacturing & Supply Company in Livermore. Two of the nineteen people on the Board were women, including prominent San Francisco resident Mrs. Louis Ghirardelli. Two members listed themselves as Capitalists, a term Phoebe had used to describe herself. Other Board members lived as far away as Hollywood and as close as Pleasanton.

As stated in the booklet, membership was perpetual, proprietary, and transferable. It could be willed or become part of the member's estate. If transferred, the new member must be approved by the Board of Directors. The roster of life members was limited to 125, and no additional life members would be accepted after the quota was complete. The initiation fee was $2,500 for life without paying any dues. "Regular members were identical, with the exception they had to pay monthly dues." Regular membership would consist of 400 people, with an initiation fee of $1,000. Prices could be increased as needed. Residency was open to people living in the following California counties: Alameda, Contra Costa, San Francisco, San Mateo, Marin, Santa Clara, Stanislaus, San Jose, and Solano. There would be no more than one hundred non-resident members, and they had to pay $500, plus monthly dues. By June 1, 1926, there were one hundred members on the roster. It's interesting to speculate how prospective members were solicited, but it should be assumed they had to be well-to-do men with fine reputations. It would also be of interest to know what criteria the Board used to qualify someone for membership. This was a very elite country club, and only the most affluent would be allowed admission.

The representations used in the booklet to describe the estate were very similar to those descriptions used when Phoebe lived there. Very eloquent language described the buildings and grounds. Photos show the exteriors and interiors of the main building,

Through the entrance gates, this view shows a 1930s car parked at the front door entrance to the Clubhouse. In the center of the courtyard is a large cement fountain, which replaced the Verona wellhead that William Hearst took to his San Simeon castle in 1920.

Late 1920s photo postcard showing the front entrance to the Clubhouse under the striped canopy. The courtyard is empty of any fountain. This is where the Verona wellhead had sat in Phoebe's day and where the Club would soon put a replacement fountain.

The same view of the courtyard, but from a different angle.

Description taken from the Club's 1926 promotional booklet: "The fine boulevards over which one motors from nearby cities to the Castlewood Country Club pass through some of the most beautiful rural scenes in California. This road enters the property."

the landscaped grounds, and forested hills. Although William R. Hearst emptied the contents of the Hacienda in 1924 when he sold it, he did leave behind $50,000 worth of furnishings and ornate wall and ceiling fixtures. An *Oakland Tribune* newspaper article confirmed this, stating, "Much of the furniture, tapestry, rugs, antiques, tables, and chairs were included in the sale." The 1926 promotional booklet mentions, "The new main building will be redecorated, furnished, and equipped as rapidly as possible and the Club will soon be fully operational."

Train transportation had always been available from Oakland to the Hacienda, with service continuing through the 1920s. The train could be ridden from Oakland, San Francisco, San Jose, Sacramento, and Stockton, the regions where membership in the Club was allowed. A Peerless Deluxe Stage also provided rides from Oakland, San Francisco, Stockton, and Livermore. The Peerless ran smoothly on thirty miles of paved highway from Oakland to Pleasanton. In those days, highways and roads were referred to as boulevards. In 1925, the new Club owners planned to have the roads "paved" from the main highway to the Castlewood property. In 1927, Foothill Road was oiled, not paved with tar, so the term "paved" probably meant oiled. A

1930s photo postcard showing the east porch at the Country Club. Table, chairs, and rocker all made of wicker.

1920 newspaper article mentions the availability of a "flying field." Eighteen members owned private airplanes, enabling them to fly in to reach Castlewood.

The clubhouse, with its fifty-three rooms, had been the central section of Phoebe's home, and it was through its massive front door where members entered. Guest rooms were immense, each decorated in a different scheme with wall coverings of silk and damask. Guests could choose to have a private bath or a connecting bath. Marble fireplaces added warmth and elegance. Every room had a telephone allowing for communication with every department of the building. A sixty-foot veranda ran along the north side of the building with its foreground sloping to botanical gardens interspersed with graveled paths leading to cozy nooks. Hundreds of tulip bulbs that had been planted in Phoebe's day bloomed in profusion during the warm season. What had been the state dining room became the Club dining room. Entrance was made through the ornate iron Cellini gate. Plush velvet rugs accented the highly polished floors. Silk tapestry draperies covered ornate window frames. Sumptuous amounts of food, attractively displayed, were served from the massive hand-carved buffet.

Because of its vast size, the music room was converted into the Club lounge. Alongside the lounge, a fifteen by fifty-one-foot glass-enclosed veranda was constructed so that members could enjoy viewing the first tee on the golf course. An ancient English warming oven made of ornamental bronze was built into the wall.

..... Scenes Ab
1. A Guest Suite in the Castle
2. Reception Hall in the Castle
3. First Fairway
4. Seventeenth Green
5. Twelfth Green
6. Ladies' Lounge in the Castle
7. East Veranda of the Castle
8. Third Green
9. Eighteenth G
10. West Verand
11. Veranda, Gue
12. Tenth Green
A Member's
at Castlewoo

1930's promotional Castlewood Country Club brochure with 19 scenes in and around the Castle. Each photo is identified as follows;

1. *A guest suite in the castle*
2. *Reception hall in the castle*
3. *First fairway*
4. *Seventeenth green*
5. *Twelfth green*
6. *Ladies' lounge in the castle*
7. *East veranda of the castle*
8. *Third green*

Description taken directly from the Club 1926 promotional booklet: "The regular dinner dances of the Club will be enjoyed in the Casino, a separate concrete building with high ceilings and special lighting effects that lend themselves felicitously to fetes, and private theatricals."

Adjoining the lounge was the library, its paneled walls made of hand-carved leather. From the lounge, members could view what had been Phoebe's ballroom surrounded by sunken gardens and huge oak trees. The ballroom became the Club casino. With its special mood lighting, it lent itself well for lavish dinner dances. Weary dancers with tired feet could sit on the veranda that wrapped around the building. From this vantage point, they could take in the panoramic landscape of the valley below. In a special building off the balcony, there were six guest rooms, each with baths and glassed-in sleeping porches. These rooms were available to party goers wishing to spend the night instead of trying to make it home after a evening of gaiety and alcohol.

The swimming pool, or plunge, as it was called, was located at the end of a long tiled promenade in the west wing of the main clubhouse. Measuring twenty feet by forty feet, the pool had its own heating plant, allowing the water to be warmed to any temperature. Its basin of soft emerald-colored tiles was filled with crystalline spring water piped from the valley. The ceilings, sidewalls, and roof were covered in glass, allowing sunlight to stream through. The grill, directly facing the ninth and eighteenth holes of the course, allowed members to eat while watching the golfers try to make their holes! What used to be Casa Bonita (the Boys' House) was now the Club's bachelor hall. Golfers could rent one of its nineteen rooms for a weekend or reside

Description taken directly from the Club's 1926 promotional booklet: "This beautiful swimming pool, twenty by forty, is an inheritance from the Hacienda. It is enclosed in glass and the pure spring water in the green-tiled basin sparkles exhilarating in the sunlight." Adjoining are commodious dressing rooms. Photo courtesy of Pleasanton's Museum on Main.

there permanently. Between 1930-1935, dinner dances were held in the downstairs part of this building. The two-story locker room building offered members the use of showers, baths, and locker quarters. This concrete building near the tennis courts and bordering the current Castlewood parking lot still stands today. Other than the poolhouse, it's the only original structure left standing from the Hacienda days.

Several service buildings were located a considerable distance from the main clubhouse. They were needed for the proper operation of Phoebe's estate, and they continued to be needed by Castlewood. There was a steam laundry for washing the bed, bath, and table linens. A dairy and creamery supplied milk products used for meals at the grill. The refrigeration plant kept food from spoiling while also supplying ice. Maintenance workers used the garage and machine shops to keep various equipment and vehicles in running order. The conservatory, an extreme area of enclosed glass, supplied flowers for the tables and plants for the gardens just as it had done

Description taken directly from the Club's 1926 promotional booklet: "Our fully equipped steam laundry, situated some distance from the main buildings, is a valuable asset to the Club. There are several service buildings."

Description taken directly from the Club's 1926 promotional booklet: "In these sumptuous stables the Piedmont Riding Academy established a riding school, and mounts and complete service are now available for members and guests at Castlewood. The equestrian is well served."

Description taken directly from the Club's 1926 promotional booklet: "The Grill, facing the ninth and eighteenth greens, is now serving members with delicious meals in a delightful setting. For polo players, equestrians returning from the hills, and especially for golfers, the Grill will be loved as a grateful oasis."

Description taken directly from the Club's 1926 promotional booklet: "This tennis court, near the Club House, is now being used by members. Additional courts will soon be under construction."

for Phoebe. Piedmont Riding Academy stabled horses for those members wishing to ride the many miles of bridle trails. The kennels had Greyhound dogs, their purpose unknown to this author. There were living accommodations for the servants and employees, the people who cooked and served the food, cleaned the rooms, and maintained the property. Housing was also provided for the many farm laborers who tended the orchards and worked the land to grow vegetables.

Water was a precious commodity and essential for Castlewood's livelihood, especially for keeping the acres of fairways green. Livermore Valley had an abundant water supply derived from deep wells, its purity and volume above average. The water supplied to Castlewood came from flowing artisan wells deep within the ground. Mrs. Hearst had entered into a contract with the Spring Valley Water Company: "An agreement in perpetuity provided that when the well water falls below a certain level, the Company shall furnish water to the property free of charge not to exceed 90 million gallons in any one year." This agreement was to stay in effect through succeeding owners of the property. The water was conveyed by pipeline over many sections of the property and apportioned so that the unusually large sprinkler and supply systems were operative. Water had to be pumped 616 feet into the hills to supply the picnic area and barbecue grounds. As quoted in the 1926 Castlewood member's booklet, "Even at such an altitude, the pressure is strong and efficient enough for fire protection. Taps are located so that connections may be made without excessive cost at almost any point within the estate." This statement would prove to be a fatal assumption when Castlewood burned to the ground in the summer of 1969 … but more on that later!

Tennis, polo, and trapshooting were offered as an alternative to golf. Due to the noise factor, trapshooting was positioned in a secluded spot far away from the hub of Club activity. Tennis courts were already in existence, but Castlewood built additional ones for the growing membership. In keeping with other Bay Area country clubs, the annual "Castlewood Cup" tennis tournament was initiated. It was the Club's intention to make Castlewood the polo headquarters of the East Bay. Located in the valley below, the polo field was very level with fine-textured soil insuring fast play; its springy consistency was excellent for the horse's footing.

The objective of the Club was to make golf the main draw. When architect William P. Bell was hired to design and construct the eighteen-hole Hillside, or "Hill" course, as it's referred to, he stated that Castlewood would be, "The only true championship course in the Bay Area." Billy Bell started in the California golf industry in 1911 as a caddie master. By the 1930s and through the 1950s, he was one of the most notable golf architects in California, having built fifty or more courses. Groundbreaking

Description taken directly from the Club's 1926 promotional booklet: "Work on the golf course is going ahead so fast that it is obviously impossible for illustrations in a printed book to keep up with it. With the progress now being made, however, the opening of the full eighteen holes for play on Labor Day 1926, is insured. Men and teams are at work on the ninth fairway." Photo courtesy of Pleasanton's Museum on Main.

and construction of the 6,502-yard course began in December 1925. At a cost of $100,000, the course was built on 150 of the 500 acres of land available. Trees from all over the world that had been planted decades before had to be removed. Twenty mule and horse teams were needed to grade and level the soil in preparation for planting the greens. The 1927 opening was held on Labor Day. With much fanfare and excitement, the crowd watched with pride as Club president, Thomas Norris, drove the first ball down the fairway. With much merriment, members and visitors celebrated the event by attending luncheons and parties that were held all day long. Now that the course was playable, the Castlewood Greens Committee proposed that three annual golf tournaments be held: the Gold Championship, the Castlewood Open, and the Annual Invitational.

To further enhance membership, the owners had always planned to add an outdoor swimming pool, and in August 1929, discussions began on building a pool. John Marshall, vice-president of Diggs & Marshall, Inc., submitted his architectural plans for construction of a pool and poolhouse. At the time, it was the largest architect company in the East Bay Area. Marshall felt that the cost of the project was the first and foremost thing to consider. Since he was already a

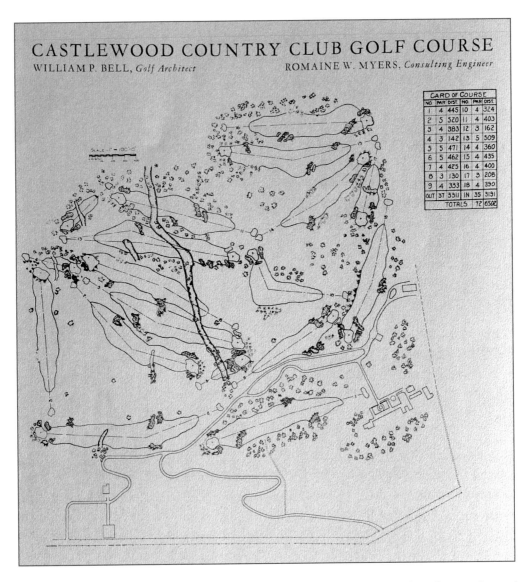

CASTLEWOOD COUNTRY CLUB GOLF COURSE

WILLIAM P. BELL, *Golf Architect*   ROMAINE W. MYERS, *Consulting Engineer*

SCALE 1" = 100'-0"

CARD OF COURSE					
NO	PAR	DIST	NO	PAR	DIST
1	4	445	10	4	324
2	5	520	11	4	403
3	4	383	12	3	162
4	3	142	13	5	509
5	4	471	14	4	360
6	5	462	15	4	435
7	4	425	16	4	400
8	3	130	17	3	208
9	4	333	18	4	390
OUT	37	3311	IN	35	3191
			TOTALS	72	6502

Image taken from the 1926 Club promotional booklet: It's captioned as the Castlewood Country Club Golf Course. William P. Bell, Golf Architect, Romaine W. Myers, Counseling Engineer. Also shows a Card of Course. Clubhouse building sketch can be seen in the lower right corner of the drawing.

lifetime member of Castlewood, he graciously offered to forgo his usual $1,500 fee for drawing the plans. Because the pool was going to be expensive, he didn't want to rush into building something just for utilitarian purposes. He wanted to keep Castlewood distinctive and different from other clubs by keeping the pool and poolhouse pleasing to the eye by having good design and construction. The original dimensions for the pool were to be fifty feet by 150 feet, but Marshall

Another version of the layout of the new golf course of 1926. Courtesy of Pleasanton's Museum on Main.

thought forty-five feet by 105 feet would be in better proportion with the surrounding Club buildings. For aesthetic purposes, he felt that the pool should run in the same direction as the causeway leading to the main clubhouse. He wanted to include the existing weeping willow tree as a superb setting for the pool, as well as for providing shade from the heat. Sadly, that tree is long gone. His plan called for the pool to be built fifteen feet below the causeway, set far away from the main buildings due to the noise factor associated with swimming pools. A pool placed in this location would eliminate the need for tearing out the existing flower beds, birch, and magnolia trees. Comfortable chairs and colorful canopied swing sets would be made available for lounging. Marshall scoffed at the idea of a two-story poolhouse. He insisted that a one-story building with dressing rooms would better serve the members. The Board was happy with his ideas, and the decision to choose Marshall as the pool architect was made. The $35,000 pool was dedicated on June 14, 1930, but the poolhouse was still under construction. For the enjoyment of the children, a sand pile, teeter-totter, and a swing and slide set were added later.

The Board of Directors thought it would be wonderful if members could live

Caption as taken from the 1926 Club promotional booklet, it describes this 1930s photo postcard: "This vista from the first tee overlooks the first fairway and the green 445 yards away. Some idea of the varied topography of the estate and its opportunities for good play may be gained by a review of the general illustrations in this book."

Opening day of the new golf course in 1926. Guests and visitors watch quietly as players ready themselves to swing their clubs.

Opening day of the new golf course in 1926. One of these men might be Club president, Thomas Norris.

Man swinging his golf club on the first tee during opening day of the new golf course in 1926. Main building of the Club is visible in the background.

392
*View of the Pool
Castlewood Country Club*

Photo postcard of the new pool completed in 1930. Shows two diving boards at the deep end, kiddie's slide and swing set in the background, two lamp posts, and the poolhouse on the right. The cement steps in the far distance are the same steps still present at today's Castlewood Country Club.

Carole MacRobert Steele

Close-up view of the new pool showing a striped canopy swing on the far right, with the Castle in the background.

The new pool showing the poolhouse and magnificent weeping willow tree. In Phoebe's day there were tennis courts at this location. The weeping willow tree was purposely left in place, rather than cut down. Folding wooden lawn chairs with striped canvas are visible in the foreground.

Vintage 1930s Castlewood Country Club matchbook featuring the pool and the Castle.

1930s view of a huge oak tree and palms. A large rustic bench under the palm tree afforded visitors a place to rest and watch golfers on the first tee. No doubt the oak tree still remains on the property.

near the golf course. They offered for sale, 220 half-acre villa sites in the "Castlewood Oaks" area. This provided members an opportunity to build private bungalows, with the revenue from the sales going directly to the Club treasury. San Francisco million-airess and Board member Mrs. Louis Ghiaradelli had a home built on one of these sites. For an interesting contrast, here are examples of home prices in the Castlewood Oaks neighborhood. In 1945, a three-bedroom, two-bath home on one acre sold for

$18,000. In 1970, a three-bedroom, three-bath home sold for $56,000. Today those same homes cost considerably more!

The Club owners could not have predicted the future, but the 1920s turned out to be a very inopportune time to start a new country club with the threat of a financial catastrophe looming on the horizon. Despite that, the Club flourished its first few years. But the stock market crash of 1929 caused even the wealthiest of the 443 members to relinquish their memberships. Because of the Depression, the Club had a difficult time maintaining itself financially. Castlewood had actually been on the verge of financial collapse since 1927. Sadly, in 1936, the mortgage on Castlewood was foreclosed on. Golf was suspended, and the polo field and gun club were shut down. On February 9, 1940, on the steps of the Anglo-California Bank in San Francisco, Castlewood was sold at a public auction to the West Coast Life Insurance Company for $185,000. Furnishings and accessories—even down to the champagne buckets—were sold at auction. Between 1936 and 1939, the name Castlewood Country Club was dropped from all signage. A billboard on Bernal Avenue in Pleasanton advertised "Castlewood Lodge" as being open to the public. It appears to have been run as a hotel from 1939-1940, where anyone could check in and spend the night. Castlewood had truly fallen from grace, but within a year, it would once again experience a rebirth that would send it in a totally new direction!

CHAPTER 5

DUDE RANCH DAYS

John Albert Marshall II was born in California in 1900. He graduated from the University of California, Berkeley in 1924 with a degree in civil engineering. Little could he have imagined how coincidental aspects of his life would be intertwined with Julia Morgan and Phoebe Hearst. He became an architect by trade, just like Julia Morgan. He was a member of a fraternity located on Hearst Avenue, and he was a student at the same university for which Phoebe had been a benefactress. How ironic that this man who would one day own the Hacienda was the same person who designed its pool and poolhouse back in 1930.

In 1931, Marshall's career interests changed when he and his wife, Edith, bought the Pyramid Lake Dude Ranch near Reno, Nevada. During this time they gained valuable experience and knowledge about dude ranch ownership and how to make it successful. In 1936, Marshall was also an organizer of the Nevada Dude Ranch Association. The skills he honed as an owner, manager, and promoter would serve him well in the years to come. In 1936 he sold the dude ranch to return to his old stomping grounds in California. In 1936, Castlewood was struggling to stay afloat. In an effort to remain solvent and gain new members, Castlewood managers made plans to make the Club more attractive by reducing their green fees and improving the buildings and equipment. Still owing $480,000, how could they make these improvements if they couldn't even make their monthly mortgage payment? Although living in Nevada, Marshall was still a lifetime Castlewood member, and he'd heard through the grapevine that Castlewood Country Club was in dire financial trouble. It was for sale with an asking price of $600,000. Because of his history with Castlewood, he knew the property had great potential. Desiring a change of scenery from the deserts of Nevada, and up for a new challenge, he made a low-ball offer of $240,000 to purchase Castlewood, which was promptly rejected. By 1940, the Club owners were anxious to unload the property and accepted Marshall's bid of $140,000 to buy Castlewood. With a $20,000 down payment, John and Edith Marshall became the new owners. Castlewood Country Club was now officially defunct, but it was about to experience huge changes under Marshall's management strategies.

The front of Old Hearst Ranch as it looked when John Marshall bought it.

Although this photo postcard is captioned Old Hearst Ranch, it's actually an early view of the Hacienda because the Verona wellhead still sits in the courtyard (removed in 1920). Although not easily visible, the winding dirt road in the valley leading from Pleasanton to the Hacienda can be seen.

Caption on this photo postcard from the 1940s reads: "Old Hearst Ranch —Pleasanton, Calif. World famous showplace at the "Tropical Paradise of the West" —Spanish castle in background —Golf course first tee at right —Tropical swimming pool at left." Causeway is now paved instead of dirt.

In a letter written by Marshall in 1975, he revealed the reason he was interested in the property: "I bought it because it was a beautiful piece of property, and country living was more healthy." He was a heavy smoker, puffing on two-to-three packs of cigarettes and five cigars a day. When they took possession of the property in 1940, it was in deplorable condition. Having sat idle and unmaintained for most of the 1930s, even the roof was almost completely gone. The golf course was badly overgrown and in need of pruning, weeding, and mowing. The liquor supply that Castlewood had purchased on a week-to-week basis was almost gone.

The Marshalls knew the dude ranch business very well, and when they opened for business in 1940, they called it "Rancho Hacienda," a resort hotel. A 1940 newspaper article referred to it as "Rancho Hacienda … former Hearst Ranch and former Castlewood Country Club." Several people kept asking Edith, "Isn't this the old Hearst ranch?" It seemed like an appropriate name for a dude ranch, so they officially changed the name to Old Hearst Ranch. Their goal was to make the Ranch easily accessible by bringing in thousands of guests by plane, train, or automobile … whatever it took! Even the Gray Line bus tours had a route to the Ranch. Their ads stated

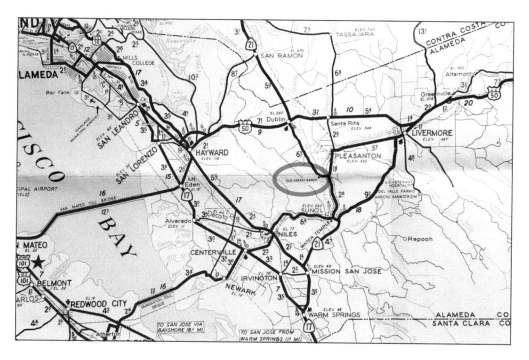

1949 map names and shows the exact location of OLD HEARST RANCH in relationship to Pleasanton and the surrounding area. Courtesy of CSAA (AAA Northern California, Nevada & Utah) copyright 1949, Bay and River Districts M-102.

that it was "one of the five leading attractions to see while visiting the San Francisco area." In the 1940s, Gray Line Tours charged $4.95, which included transportation, dinner, a swim, and the opportunity to participate in the live radio show broadcast on KFSO in San Francisco. Sponsored by General Mills, the program was called *Live Like A Millionaire* and was broadcast on more than seventy-three radio stations. If a person wanted to make a reservation for a stay at the Ranch, the phone number to call was Pleasanton 2233. A taxi cab ride from Pleasanton was only a five-minute ride. Although 150 property owners protested against it, in 1949 Old Hearst Ranch had its own airport. Flight instructor Harry Lustig was granted permission to build the $50,000 Pleasanton Airport with its 1,400-foot runway.

Old Hearst Ranch almost became the "Pop" Warner Dude Ranch. In 1939-40, the Stanford University football coach collaborated with John Marshall about buying the property. They couldn't agree on a price, so Pop let John have it … and the rest is history! While in the Bay Area, leading football teams made the Ranch their head-quarters to relax and practice before playing games in nearby San Francisco.

During the years of World War II, the Ranch made very little money. The facil-ities were in poor condition because materials were hard to come by to make the needed repairs. Wages and salaries were frozen at low figures, and gas and food were

Old Hearst Ranch • PLEASANTON, CALIFORNIA
"World's Largest and Most Popular Dude Ranch"

Late 1940s postcard epitomizes life at Old Hearst Ranch—World's Largest and Most Popular Dude Ranch. This image appears in the 1940s Ranch promotional brochure and is captioned as follows: "Smiling sunny summer skies. Such super fun soaking up the noonday sun, for our beautiful sun-bronzed goddesses and handsome Adonises. Tropical turquoise pool. Swimming and sunning in one of the finest pools under the sun –and in water as pure as you drink. A beautiful location in the hollow, graduating depth and crystal-clear water, changing twice daily. You will enjoy peaceful, happy hours, under a lazy sun, building up a reserve of energy, acquiring a glamor-tan, soaking up sunshine and health. Rx –sunshine (vitamin D) soothes tired nerves, buildings healthy bodies."

rationed. When the war was over, they doubled the number of rooms, increasing the occupancy to accommodate 250 vacationers. Casa Bonita (the Boys' House) was also utilized to provide additional guest rooms. The Marshalls made improvements by putting in a new kitchen, a dining room, four bars, and extra bathrooms. A large outdoor barbecue and dining area were also built. An attractive dancing spot was added, which they called the Palm Pool Patio. By the late 1940s and into the 1950s, the Ranch was declared, "The world's largest and most popular dude ranch." The Marshalls added so many amenities that *Glamour Magazine* proclaimed, "We have chosen Old Hearst Ranch as one of the ten most popular resorts throughout the country." In 1944, there were 55,000 visitors and guests.

The Ranch was thoroughly modern and equipped with: electric lighting, refrigeration, steam heat, telephones, wire service, daily mail and newspapers, candy, cigarettes, postcards, playing cards, souvenirs, and novelties. For twenty-five cents, a souvenir

Photo postcard from the late 1940s captioned on front: "At times thousands daily. Photo shows overflow parking on golf course." In addition: "During the past three years, the Ranch has probably had more visitors and guests than any other western resort or dude ranch." Glamour Magazine writes: "We have chosen the Old Hearst Ranch as one of the ten most popular resorts throughout the country." This view is actually the first fairway and I'm surprised they would have allowed cars onto the greens! The cactus in the foreground was probably superimposed by the photographer.

brochure depicting the Ranch could be bought. With no fog and temperatures no hotter than eighty-five degrees, it was open from April through October, offering vacationers and day visitors a lively and invigorating array of activities. Meals were available from the Tropical Dining Room, where guests could eat in the patio area among lush palm and cactus gardens. The menu included everything from pickled pigs feet to Louisiana prawns. Wonderfully prepared and deliciously delightful drinks were served in the Celebrity Bar adjoining the Tropical Dining Room. It was called the Celebrity Bar because of the numerous celebrity photographs displayed on its walls. Non-alcoholic drinks were available at the Coke Bar and Fountain.

The Marshalls did not allow guests to bring in liquor from the outside. That's why the bars were always stocked with favorite brands to satisfy every taste. The Ranch served its own specialty cocktails with secret ingredients and embellished with winsome garnishes. These drinks included: "California Sunshine" (non-alcoholic), "Moonshine," and "Old Hearst Ranch Punch" made with rum. Always the

Late 1940s view of huge crowds at the pool. The occasion is unknown.

great promoter, Marshall even produced his own brand of whiskey called O.H.R. Whiskey. It was bottled exclusively by American Distribution Company in Sausalito, California. This company had once been the world's largest independent producers of whiskey and vodka. It's believed that in the 1920s, there was a bootlegger's drop spot located in the brick wine cellar behind the current upper Castlewood parking lot. A tunnel that ran under the parking lot connected to a depository in the clubhouse. An underground wine cave was used for storing wine at a perfect temperature.

For those wanting a quick meal, the coffee shop served breakfast, snacks, and soft drinks and was open from 8 a.m. until 11 p.m. The Round-Up Room was another popular dining spot, decorated ranch-style with actual western cattle brands burned into the walls. Hot and hungry swimmers and sunbathers could order hot dogs, cold drinks, and ice cream at the pool La Cantina. Sunday was a busy day at the Ranch. It was the scene of the *Sunday Breakfast* live radio show, which was located off the hotel lobby. There were so many activities to choose from, but not to be missed was the popular western barbecue served with all the trimmings. For added fun and entertainment, twenty-four gaily-costumed dancers from the California Folk Dancing Federation put on exhibitions. Other activities included dancing under a canopy of palms, or standing by the outdoor fireplace to keep warm on cool evenings. Patrons could watch a movie, dive into the pool for a night swim, or go for a horse-drawn hayride, eat hot dogs at the wiener roast, or attend the Ranch foreman's cocktail party.

Carole MacRobert Steele

The cover of a late 1940s Old Hearst Ranch promotional brochure. Caption inside the brochure reads: "Fabulous, historic 2½ million dollar early California hacienda —where kings and queens have been entertained. World's largest and most popular dude ranch. Breathtaking beauty in a tropical setting of palm trees, exotic flowers, cactus gardens. Famous for fun, sun, fine food and friendly feeling. Maximum vacation enjoyment, barbecues, hayrides, swim, golf, ranch games, cocktails, dance under the stars." Photos inside the brochure depict several of the same photos seen in this book because the Marshalls used the brochure photos to make souvenir postcards for mailing.

Other entertainment might include: ping pong, billiards, card games, storytelling, and singing. If dancing was a desired activity, guests could waltz under the stars at the Palm Pool Patio or swing their partners to and fro to the music of fiddle and accordion players at the barn dance. People with or without talent, could join in on "Amateur Night" to try and win prizes for the best act. Wranglers were on hand every day to guide and teach those wanting to go horseback riding on the numerous bridle trails leading into the nearby hills. These trails had existed since Phoebe days. Both gentle and spirited mounts could be rented for $1.50 an hour. For the less energetic, the Sun Garden was built for fresh air addicts and sun-worshipers to lounge and luxuriate in comfort.

Guests could always count on excellent food, comfortable beds, and a clean environment. Day visitors were welcome to dine, drink at the bars, or participate in sports, but they had to exit the Ranch premises by midnight. If they wanted to stay longer, they could rent rooms by the week or month, or stay only a few days. Room rates, some with private bath, cost $8.75 to $19 a day, depending on the type of accommodation needed. Those rates included a room and two meals, with no extra charge for activities. Apparently dogs found the pool irresistible, so Rover had to stay home. Nineteen fifty-one proved to be a banner year when 143 couples honeymooned

Help Yourself –All You Can Eat. This late 1940s postcard is captioned on backside: "Hawaiian Dining Room –South Seas atmosphere, candlelight, palm trees, music. Dinners include selection of assorted delicacies from Hors d'Oeuvre Bar. (Balance of meal, including entree, dessert, beverage, served by waitresses.) Jams, jellies, Kona coffee, poi from Hawaii –Scandinavian imports –select California specialties –served in unique museum piece collection of bowls and platters, recently brought from South Sea Islands –hand-carved by natives from monkey pod, koa, milo woods, in shapes of turtles, pineapples, tropical fish, etc. Chef Larry in charge for eight years." (Diego Rivera mural can be seen on the wall behind the buffet).

Late 1940s postcard: "Western barbecue dinner with all the trimmings on the Sunview Terrace. Inspiring view of the valley below. Outdoor fireplace –barbecue pit –palm frond canopy. Buckaroo Bar (on right) for private parties. Large capacity. Shaded by two huge Cedars of Lebanon, planted by Luther Burbank, who brought the trees from the Holy Land fifty years ago." Every Sunday morning at 9:30, radio station KSFO ran the "Dude Ranch Breakfast Show" from the Old Hearst Ranch.

Late 1940s postcard shows the Palm Pool Patio tropical lanai –the new outdoor patio. Card captioned on backside as: "The lanai having delicate wrought-iron work, grilled archways, exotic plants and flowers. Dancing under the stars to the soft strains of melodious music, beside a tinkling fountain. Flattering indirect night-lighting in the tropical foliage. Dubonnet Dance Orchestra every night."

Image from the late 1940s shows: "The largest attendance of 893 people at the Dude Ranch breakfast and radio show –held every Sunday morning –Breakfast 10:00 a.m. – Entertainment 11:00 –Radio Show –11:30 –Listen to re-broadcast the following Sunday morning –9:30 KSFO. A delightfully different and popular program. Out-of-doors on the Valley View Terrace, just off the lobby, in the healthful California sunshine. Radio stars –celebrities, audience participation –prizes, fun for everyone. At the West's Largest and Most Popular Dude Ranch."

Late 1940s postcard captioned on front: "Castle Entrance Courtyard. Tropical setting – sunshine, green lawns and palm trees. Old Hearst Ranch, Pleasanton, Calif." Two costumed waitresses stand by an iron gate."

Late 1940s postcard captioned on front as the tropical lanai. Two gaily costumed waitresses sit under the umbrella at the table. A white fountain is visible between the large plant on the left and the ladies.

Carole MacRobert Steele

This superb photo of the pool and La Cantina shows the magnificent weeping willow tree with its branches hanging low on the red tiled roof. The pool was designed around the willow so the tree could be saved. The tree was still alive in the 1950s, but is long since gone. The pool and poolhouse design was started by John Marshall in 1929 and completed in 1930. The pool measured fifty feet by one-hundred and forty feet and could be heated to any desired temperature. The La Cantina had dressing rooms with showers. Photo courtesy of Pleasanton's Museum on Main.

Author took this photo in 2013. It shows the original wine cellar dating from Phoebe's day. It's located on a back road directly off of Castlewood's main entrance parking lot.

Barbecue on View Terrace overlooking the Livermore Valley. Postmarked 1947.

Western barbecue dinner on Sun View Terrace overlooking the Livermore Valley. Postmarked 1947.

Carole MacRobert Steele

Late 1940s scene of the View Terrace barbecue and picnic grounds where thousands of people have been entertained, set high in the hills overlooking Livermore Valley. Men wearing chefs hats and aprons are seen cooking at the barbecue pit as people stand in line waiting to be served.

Late 1940s couples dancing on the Valley View Terrace overlooking the Livermore Valley.

Late 1940s scene of "Dudes playing cowboy heading for the Ranch Roundup in the 'Cocktail Corral.' Only by riding over its miles of beautiful bridle paths could one appreciate how refreshingly varied are the aspects that gave a tireless charm to Old Hearst Ranch."

This is an actual six of diamonds Old Hearst Ranch playing card. Words on the front include: "The West's Most Glamorous Dude Ranch."

Carole MacRobert Steele

Postmarked 1948, sender writes, "Dear Family, Eating breakfast outside in a patio overlooking the valley with a view like the one on this card. They have a broadcast every Sun. morning from here given for the guests while eating breakfast. Going horseback riding now." The 1950s Old Hearst Ranch brochure describes horseback riding on lazy summer days as follows: "Ride the romantic rancho range like the caballeros of early days over hill and valley. A fine string of gentle and spirited horses. Genial helpful Steve Fuller and his dude wranglers on hand to guide and instruct you. Group riding $1.50 an hour." Directly in front of these riders is the golf course with the swimming pool and Hacienda.

at Old Hearst Ranch. Casual clothing was the mode of the day: blue jeans matched with a brightly patterned western shirt, sports clothes, sun and swimsuits; however, swimsuits were not allowed to be worn inside the Hacienda's main building. That's why dressing rooms were provided at the pool area.

From promotion tactics learned from his days at Pyramid Lake, Marshall spent $32,000 for Ranch advertising in just six months. For sketching guest portraits, Don McFadden was hired as Ranch artist. Or, if a guest preferred, he or she could have his or her photo taken while seated in a huge peacock chair, or some other glamorous setting. The photo was mounted on the inside of a thick six-inch by eight-inch folder. The folder's outside cover featured a color view of the Ranch with the words: "We sincerely hope you have an enjoyable stay with us at the Old Hearst Ranch." The folder, with photo, was mailed to the guest's home, and additional copies could be bought by contacting Sterling Photography Company, in care of Old Hearst Ranch, Pleasanton, California. Marshall arranged for famous Mexican artist Diego Rivera to paint murals for the Celebrity Bar. In a self-portrait located behind the bar, Rivera

Old Hearst Ranch • PLEASANTON, CALIFORNIA
"World's Largest and Most Popular Dude Ranch"

Busy day at the pool as the Ranch's 1940s brochure describes: "Country fun in the sun. Here at this glorious background you will meet a grand group of congenial companions and pack every hour with enjoyment. Never a dull moment for the ranch and country provide a wide variety of things to do to suit your whims and inclination. Yes, even the children have their sand pile, teeters, swings and slide (swings for the grownups too.)" In the foreground you can see the children on the teeter-totter.

OLD HEARST RANCH
Play like a king on 2½
million dollar dude ranch.

Zan 493

Late 1940s captioned: "Play like a king on 2½ million dollar dude ranch."

Carole MacRobert Steele

This vintage 1950s Old Hearst Ranch matchbook shows an image of the pool and poolhouse. Also shows a little map of its location and how many miles it is from various nearby cities. On the inside it lists all the attributes of the Ranch and is signed John Albert Marshall II, manager-owner for ten years.

OLD HEARST RANCH, Pleasanton, Calif.
Country fun in the sun.
Roam over 500 acres of
wooded and view trails.

Ian 494

Late 1940s captioned on front: "Country fun in the sun. Roam over 500 acres of wooded and view trails." Quoted from the 1950s brochure: "World famous 'showplace' romantically reminiscent of the glorious days of the dons; outstanding example of old Spanish Hacienda. An extensive rancho, carefully and gradually developed through the years to a point where it is now the only one of its kind —and one which could not be duplicated."

Early 1950s captioned on front: "Golfer's Paradise! Imagine golf on a dude ranch –yes, and on one of the finest courses in the U. S.; 18 holes, easy to play, broad all-grass fairways, velvet greens, spectacular view, first (above) and new tenth tees within 300 feet of the Hacienda. Golf pro, lessons, clubs rented, games arranged for those who come alone, tournaments."

1940s country fun in the sun. First tee of eighteen-hole golf course near Castle entrance. Old Hearst Ranch.

Late 1940s shows two lady golfers on this eighteen-hole championship course, rated fifth best in the U. S. The first fairway (as shown) is one hundred yards from the Old Hearst Ranch entrance.

Carole MacRobert Steele

1940s captioned on front of postcard: "Golf and swim for vigor and vim. Old Hearst Ranch." Man relaxes on a bench under the tree on the left. Nearby is a drinking fountain. There is also a park bench for golfers to sit while waiting their turn.

1940s with caption: "18 hole golf course; rated 5th best in U.S." This is actually the ninth and eighteenth greens with the Castle in the background.

When Phoebe lived at the Hacienda, this room was the Main Hall. Old Hearst Ranch used it as the entrance lobby and reception desk. The caption on this late 1940s postcard reads in part: "World Famous Show Place—where kings and queens and great artists have been entertained. Three generations of the Hearst family have made this their home." Photo shows the reception desk, just inside the Castle entrance. In addition, these words are taken from the 1940s promotional Ranch brochure: "Ranch Hacienda tour; interesting short walking trip around Hacienda and points of interest; old underground wine cave; red velvet walled State Dining Room; historical California Room with its leaded windows made from champagne bottle bottoms, where great artists entertained—Paderewski, Galli-Curci, Schumann, Heinck, Caruso, Madame Tetrazzini. No charge or tipping."(Notice the fireplace on the left wall.)

can be seen as a prominent figure in a Hawaiian luau scene. Rivera was born in Mexico in 1886 and died in 1957. He studied the post-impressionism style of art in Spain and Paris.

The Marshalls traveled the world in search of new ideas to better their hotel operation and expand the unique food offerings. While dining in the exotic destinations of Singapore, Budapest, Bombay, Hawaii, Naples, Cuba, and Paris, they were able to sample a wide variety of edibles. At the Ranch, displayed under protective glass, were menus John had collected from all these foreign locations.

The Marshalls' philosophy of running a successful dude ranch was to do all their own advertising aimed at repeat local patronage. Their goal was to satisfy the locals with good food and good service. The rooms had to be in good repair and attractively

This is the bar where my Dad bought me my first "Shirley Temple" drink. This late 1940s postcard is captioned on back as being the Celebrity Bar —"A romantic rendezvous in an atmosphere tropical and glamorous. Hard liquor and soft music —old wines and young fun. Featuring beautiful Diego Rivera mural and signed photographs of celebrities. Presided over by Ray Abadilla, outstanding mixologist and authority on tropical drinks." The 1940s Ranch brochure describes this bar as having: "Soft colorful lighting, tropical garden effect with indoor planting. Presided over by Johnnie Cruz, outstanding mixologist …" The man behind the bar is either Ray or Johnnie! Also from this brochure it states that the "Diego Rivera mural by one of the world's foremost artists painted especially for the Ranch Celebrity Bar. Colorful Hawaiian luau (feast) scene in which the artist himself is a dominant figure. This mural was painted at historic Angel Inn in the Villa Obregon Colony of Mexico City, December, 1944."

decorated. The grounds, driveway, and patio were enhanced with bright and colorful flowers. At night, the buildings were illuminated with pastel lighting, emitting an "enchanted fairyland of colors." All this was done in an effort to keep up the appeal, and in response, 150 different local organizations held their functions at the Ranch.

In 1952, there was an average of 110 employees, mostly from the local area, who worked part-time at the Ranch. If they had no means of transportation, the Marshalls paid their taxi fares so they could get to work. John and Edith ran a tight ship, demanding complete honesty and loyalty. If employees were stealing the silver, they wanted to know! In the days when the Ranch was Castlewood Country Club, rumors spread that it was honeycombed with secret passages and two-way mirrors for

Inside the image (postcard text):

Merry Christmas FROM *Edith and John Marshall* IN HAWAII (just looking around for ideas to try out on you next year)

OLD HEARST RANCH, Pleasanton, Calif. World's largest and most popular dude ranch. Famous 2½ million dollar early Calif. Hacienda, where kings and queens have been entertained — Breath-taking beauty, and a "MUST SEE" for all California visitors. Tropical setting of palm trees, cactus gardens. Superb meals. "Where the sun shines all the time" — just 36 miles from San Francisco. Open April 15 to Oct 15, 1950.

This photo postcard is postmarked from Honolulu, Hawaii, December 31, 1949, and shows John and Edith (circled) at a luau in Hawaii. Caption reads: "Merry Christmas from Edith and John Marshall in Hawaii (just looking around for ideas to try out on you next year)." The larger caption on the postcard says the Ranch will be open April 15 to October 15, 1950. The following description of the Marshalls as written in the 1940s Ranch brochure: "Edith and John Marshall of the Ranch, go thousands of miles yearly in search of ideas on hotel operation and foods, sampling mixed grills in Buenos Aires, rijsttafel in Singapore, goulashes of Budapest, flaming sword dinners in Chicago, Indian curries in Bombay, pipikaula and poi in Hawaii, manicotti Vesuvius in Naples, paella in Havana, crepes suzette in Paris, pompano en papillote in New Orleans."

the purpose of spying on guests and staff. This monitoring could have started back in the Phoebe days. It would be like her to do something like this.

It was fun and exciting for the Marshalls to entertain celebrities such as Clark Gable, Zane Grey, Alan Ladd, Eleanor Roosevelt, and others. Meeting these stars was an added perk to the ranch life they loved, but they'd reached an age when they were ready to retire. By the early 1950s, the popularity of western dude ranches was slowing declining. John and Edith decided to sell the Ranch, keeping twenty acres for themselves on which to build their dream home.

Construction of the pink Mediterranean style villa at 70 Castlewood Drive took seven years to complete. It was located high on a hill overlooking Old Hearst Ranch and golf course. They named their new home Villa del Sol, "House of the Sun." I have a clear childhood memory of this huge house on a distant hill. It was quite an

Shows an air view of Old Hearst Ranch at the height of its popularity in the late 1940s. The willow tree by the poolhouse must have died in the 1930s or early 1940s because it's not seen in this view. Perhaps disrupting the ground during the building of the poolhouse had a detrimental effect on the health of the tree, causing it to die.

eye-catcher with its bright pink color contrasted against a background of blue sky and green-forested hills.

They decorated and furnished their mansion extravagantly. Each bedroom was given a name: the Gold Room, the Copper Room, and the Jade Room, reflecting the color, objects, and decor specific to that room. John hand-carved the ornate doors and master bedroom headboard. Because of the theme of the house, appropriately placed sun symbols graced the fireplace and doorways throughout the home. Having a swimming pool was a must. It was included in the landscape planning, along with 4,000 plants of various species. Perhaps it was their intention, but when the home and landscaping were completed, it looked very similar to Phoebe's Hacienda. John lovingly worked on their "House of the Sun" up until his death. They kept mementos from the Hearst Hacienda, including hundreds of photographs taken when it was a country club in the 1930s. In the 1950s, Castlewood Club management wanted John to set up an exhibit of photos, but he refused to do so until adequate fire protection could be assured. The Marshalls also owned items belonging to Phoebe: a 1903 Christmas card, stationery, a hand-embroidered letter case, and a hand-painted parchment depicting horse and buggy days, which had hung over the fireplace in the

Hacienda entrance hall. Other items from Phoebe's Hacienda that graced their new home were: upholstered dining room furniture, various pieces of carved furniture, ornate wall panels, and iron gates. The Marshalls were acquaintances of William R. Hearst, and in 1945, they received an invitation to visit him at his home in San Simeon. Perhaps their friendship with him was the reason why they were able to acquire so many of Phoebe's belongings

After leading a very full and active life, John Marshall died from a heart attack in 1976. He had first visited Pleasanton in 1906 when he was a child traveling with his father. They needed a room for the night and stayed at the Pleasanton Hotel. John's obituary ran on February 26, 1976, in the *Hayward Daily Review* with the heading, "Prominent Pleasanton Man Dies." Edith was born in 1911 and died in 2000. Both are buried at the I.O.O.F. Memory Gardens Cemetery in Livermore, California.

CHAPTER 6

THE REBIRTH OF CASTLEWOOD COUNTRY CLUB

BORN IN 1911, LAURENCE "LARRY" CURTOLA WORKED AT THE SHIP-yards in Vallejo, California, during World War II. Additionally, he was a restauranteur, property developer, and builder. He was a talented man and well known for being an expert golf course designer. In 1952, he had just finished renovating Diablo Country Club in Oakland, California, (which he owned), when he heard the news that the Old Hearst Ranch was for sale. With postwar prosperity at a high, he sensed it was a good time to consider purchasing the Ranch. Larry and his brother Ronald enlisted five other San Francisco Bay Area businessmen to go in on the purchase. Among those five men was future San Francisco Mayor Joseph Alioto (1966-73). On November 14, 1952, these entrepreneurs spent $1,000,000 to buy and develop the existing buildings and 224 acres. When John Marshall sold it to them, he "threw" in the land for $500 an acre. By 1966, building sites near Castlewood were selling for $75,000 an acre! The Club had reclaimed its name and was on its way back to being the upscale country club that it had been in the 1920s. Its new motto was, "Luxury at a price low enough to be within the budget of the average family." In the 1920s, the Club had targeted only a wealthy clientele.

The property needed the three R's: renovation, restoration, and reclamation. With this plan in mind, work started immediately on restoring the buildings and organizing lavish events to attract new members. When the renovations were taking place, construction workers discovered the indoor pool that had been covered up during the Old Hearst Ranch era. It was the same glorious pool that Phoebe had built early in the century. The pool would now become part of the mens' locker room. Curtola built the Colonnade Room to replace the existing eastern verandas. This room could seat 250 people for dining. In addition, a separate banquet room was built to accommodate up to 600.

1950s view of the front of the Hacienda now with white posts keeping cars from entering. There are two posted signs. The one on the left has an arrow pointing to the Locker Room Parking –Members Only and the sign on the right has an arrow pointing to the Main Parking Area.

The Hill Course, finished in 1927, was restored to its previous condition, and the holes were realigned; still existing as they are today. In the early 1950s, the popularity of golf was at an all time high. To meet the demands of its members, Club managers agreed that more course space was needed. To accomplish this, Larry Curtola designed and constructed the Valley Course located east of Foothill Road. What had been Phoebe's acres of orchards, vineyard, gardens, and 1,000 avocado trees was bulldozed to make way for the new course. The gun and polo clubs, train station, and airport were also removed. Excitement grew as the new course began to take shape, and in 1954, it was completed. Famous golf professional Byron Nelson was on hand for the inauguration. Castlewood Country Club could now take claim to having a course with thirty-six holes!

Phoebe may or may not have liked or understood golf, but she certainly wouldn't have been happy to see her orchards torn out. Because golf brought enjoyment to so many people, she would have been content with that. It was not long before membership reached 1,000 with another 370 on a waiting list. Even in the early days of its reopening, there were whispered rumors that Castlewood could someday be bought by its members, and those rumors would come to pass. In 1954, Curtola was leasing the property to the membership for a ten-year period, with an option to buy for $1.25 million. In 1960, Castlewood was flourishing; boasting an appraised

This is a 1970s Castlewood Country Club men's and women's golf score card. Shows the newly built clubhouse and Hill Course layout. Card folds open for players to write down their scores. U.S.G.A. and Club regulations are printed on the backside.

value of $2 million. The membership voted to initiate their option of buying out the current owners. Weeks earlier, all the members had been mailed a questionnaire concerning this option, and the majority voted in favor of it. This meant that the future of the Club would be kept stable and in the hands of people who truly loved it. The $1.25 million sale was finalized in 1961. Two golf courses, all roads, sewer and water systems, pool, grounds, parking areas, main clubhouse, and all other buildings were included in the purchase price. After the sale was completed, Curtola moved on to other successful ventures while his brother, Ron, stayed on as Castlewood's manager for the next twenty years.

The Club, now under member ownership, did very well through the 1960s as golf tournaments grew in popularity. Because of the new heightened interest, women's golf was also being heavily promoted. In 1961, there was talk of expansion, including more tennis courts. The last year of the decade, however, would prove disastrous for this eighty-year old historic property that had survived so many changes. In the summer of 1969, Phoebe was weeping in heaven.

"Ashes to ashes … dust to dust …" Ashes and dust were all that was left of Castlewood Country Club on the evening of August 24, 1969. A poem written in 1969

Castlewood's matchbooks went through design changes through the years. These range from the 1940s (green one) to the 1970s (yellow one). All three have the same Club logo symbols inside the crest.

Carole MacRobert Steele

(author unknown) emotes the sense of loss:

There's nothing left but the ashes
and memories each will recall.
There lies the grand Hacienda
flames have demolished it all.
Created for living and pleasure,
symbols of one woman's home.
Can we rebuild all its splendor
from total destruction reclaim.

It was a warm and windless August evening. John and Edith Marshall had just said goodnight to the last of their guests after hosting a pleasant evening dining outdoors during their annual Full Moon Harvest Festival. At 10:30 p.m., Edith sat at her kitchen table overlooking Castlewood. She was signing her name to a check, paying the woman she'd hired to help with the party. The silence of that solitary act was broken by the wailing of nearby sirens. Edith's heart raced and fear crept into her mind as the disconcerting sound drew closer. She and her husband watched in horror as flames shot from the towers of the Hacienda below. Just twenty minutes prior to seeing the flames, Edith observed that everything at Castlewood looked fine and calm, but now the aroma of smoke filled the air as the crackling sound of fire echoed all around. The beloved Hacienda they had once owned and lived in was being consumed in a blazing firestorm.

Interviewed by newspaper reporters the day after the fire, Edith stated, "All the years we owned it, we had been worried about the possibility of fire." She continued to say, "It looked like daylight; the building was completely engulfed in flames … the fire lit up the sky." With great sadness in her voice, she uttered her final words about the disaster, "The beautiful old place and all its treasures and art objects vanished in all the flames." John added his solemn impression, "We knew it was just as dry as tinder." With a heavy heart, he expressed, "It was horrible. It's a tremendous shock." When asked about the fire, Ken Burge, former Castlewood Club president said, "There goes the last of the Queens."

The night of the fire, Castlewood was closed after having been open all day for a social event, but now the fire was well under way and spreading fast. Several husband and wife teams lived and worked at Castlewood, but this night, there were only two people at the Club when the blaze started, the night watchman and the dishwasher. Ordinarily, a staff of seventy-five employees kept the Club running, and up to 125 were used when there was a large banquet. When interviewed, the dishwasher, who

Castlewood Country Club as it looked about the time the Marshalls sold it as a dude ranch and it reverted back to being a country club. Courtesy of Pleasanton's Museum on Main.

had been cleaning up after the day's event, stated that he saw flames shooting up the wall of the vacant mens' locker room, and that he and the watchman had tried to fight the flames with a fire extinguisher. This action caused them to lose valuable time that should have been spent calling the fire department, but even an early call wasn't going to save the landmark from total destruction.

Gene Marsh, a resident living near the entrance gate on Castlewood Drive, was the first person to make the fire call. His wife was driving home after attending a social function, and from the freeway, her eye caught sight of flames darting from two windows above the locker room. Arriving home in a state of panic, she breathlessly told her husband what she'd seen. He immediately rushed to the Club to investigate. Entering the smoke-filled lobby, he tried in vain to call the fire department, but was forced to retreat by crawling on his hands and knees through the thick smoke, seeking the safety of the outdoors.

Castlewood had a fire protection contract with the Pleasanton Fire Department. According to their records, the first alarm was called in at 10:20 p.m. The second

John and Edith Marshall as they appeared on the night Castlewood Country Club burned to the ground August 24, 1969. Dressed in typical Ranch attire, the Marshalls stand by picnic tables set and ready for guests to arrive for their annual Full Moon Harvest Festival dinner. John holds a squash and Edith holds a jar of preserves. The checker-clothed table tops are laden with jars of preserved foods and fresh vegetables. Candles and lanterns are present to provide light when the evening darkened. The vast and somewhat barren Livermore Valley lay in the background with the Country Club below, but not visible in this photo. However, from this vantage point on their terrace, the Marshalls could easily see the Club just below their home on this hill. Their otherwise happy event would end with great heartache. Photo courtesy of Pleasanton's Museum on Main.

alarm was called at 10:28 p.m., and the third alarm was called at 10:57 p.m. Once the firemen surveyed the scene and determined a plan of action, their main goal was to save the music room and the Club office. Flames stopped just a few feet short of the office vault, preventing tens of thousands of dollars of accounts receivable from burning up. Thanks to their professionalism, the firemen were able to save the music room, the Club office, the ladies' locker room, and the pro-golf shop. All that remained of the structure were two chimneys and a few blackened stucco walls. Because Casa Bonita was far from the proximity of the blaze, it was not affected. A total of eleven fire departments and other agencies from the surrounding area arrived

The view that greeted visitors as they walked through the gates of Castlewood the day after the fire: the remains of a charred and crumbling chimney with a beautiful fountain left unharmed. Photo courtesy of Pleasanton's Museum on Main.

Carole MacRobert Steele

to find the structure fully engulfed. Thirty pieces of equipment were used as eighty-three men from thirty units fought valiantly for three hours to save what they could of this beloved landmark.

In February 2015, I had an opportunity to interview Terry Burt, who had gotten a first-hand account of the fire from his boss, the watchman on duty the night of the fire at Castlewood, and the last person to leave the burning building. In 1969, Burt was a twenty-two-year-old security guard working for the Hayward Industrial Security Police. The night of the fire, he was on duty at the General Electric Research Lab. From one-and-a-half miles away, looking across the freeway in the direction of Castlewood, he saw a "ball of flame" and lots of smoke. Castlewood was on fire! Even from his location, he could hear loud popping noises as the windows at Castlewood blew out. Describing what he remembered, he stated, "The fire burned very fast … it went up like cardboard."

Burt's boss, a sergeant with the Hayward Industrial Security Police, was on duty at Castlewood as the night watchman. His recollection (as told to Burt), was that a social event was in progress in the banquet room. At the west end of the building, he climbed the stairs for his routine inspection of the twelve-to-fourteen upper story guest rooms. When he touched the door of the stairwell to enter the hall, it was "red hot" with a lot of smoke coming from beneath the door. Thanks to training he had received, he knew better than to open the door! Luckily, no one was staying in the rooms, and no people had been booked for the month of August. Alarmed at what was happening, he frantically ran down the stairs passing the kitchen on the way. He yelled to the cook to "shut off the stove gas valve." He hurried to the banquet room to the people enjoying their party and yelled to them to "get out and grab whatever you can." The nervous guests fled; taking pictures off the walls, grabbing small furniture and other precious objects as they rushed toward the door of the reception lobby. His job training had taught him that he was always to be the last man out—that it was his duty to make sure everyone got out of the building safely before he was free to leave.

The day after the fire, the site needed twenty-four-hour security to keep bystanders away from the dangerous area. It was probably considered a crime scene and an arson investigation would need to be performed to determine the cause and origin of the fire. The following day, Burt was assigned to a twelve-hour shift to stand guard at the entrance to Castlewood to keep curious onlookers from entering. When he showed up for duty, he had a chance to talk with his sergeant (the night watchman) about what happened the previous night. The sergeant related to Burt the circumstances under which he discovered the fire, and the actions he had taken, adding that he did not call the fire department. He said the smoke had a distinct electrical fire smell. In Burt's

Crowd of onlookers the day after the fire staring in disbelief at the smoldering remains of their beloved landmark. This view shows the entrance gates and a fire engine to the right. Courtesy of Castlewood Country Club.

A lone woman stands before the ruins of the once grand Hacienda. She looks bewildered and bereaved by the sight of the fallen and blackened walls. This was a dangerous area the day after the fire and curious and concerned visitors were discouraged from trying to visit. Guards were posted to keep them out. Courtesy of Castlewood Country Club.

Professional and volunteer firemen came from miles around to try and put out the fire, but it was too intense and had started to burn long before they had a chance to arrive. This view through the front gates show the firemen managing dozens of hoses as they try to shoot water on the voracious flames that engulfed and destroyed the entire Hacienda. Courtesy of Pleasanton's Museum on Main and Livermore Heritage Guild.

memory, the first fire engine on the scene came from nearby Niles Canyon. He also mentioned that there may have been a thermostatically controlled fire alarm on the front of the building, which may have gone off, thereby alerting the fire department of the emergency. The sergeant continued his story by describing how the party-goers ran from the building. They crowded by the front gate out of concern for the safety of their cars parked nearby. Two Pleasanton police cars were on site, but they had to park off the road so they wouldn't impede the several fire trucks that were hastily

Several large red clay pots remained unharmed after the Hacienda fire. Colorful flowers contained in the pots were a stark contrast to the blackened rubble of the fallen walls shown in this photo. These clay pots were saved and used again when the new Castlewood Country Club was rebuilt a couple of years later. A man stands nearby looking in disbelief at the sight before him. Courtesy of Castlewood Country Club.

enroute. That evening, news of the fire spread quickly as onlookers arrived weeping openly as the stucco walls fell, one by one. The third-story rooms that had once been William Hearst's were now gone. Castlewood had reverently maintained them in their original condition, and the Club staff had cynically referred to them as the "wasteful Willie rooms."

Several factors contributed to how and why the fire spread so quickly. One of the main reasons was that the buildings had been constructed using balloon framing, where wall studs extended from the sill of the first story and all the way to the top-end rafter of the second story. One of the disadvantages of using balloon framing is that it creates a path for fire to readily travel from floor to floor. Ordinarily, firestops (places where openings and joints are sealed) are used at each floor level to prevent fire from spreading. When the home was constructed, this was not done; therefore,

Smoke from the ruins is visible through these charred pillars that once held strong white walls. The debris continued to smolder for several days. A warning sign is posted on the wall on the right. Chunks of broken stucco lay in the foreground. Courtesy of Castlewood Country Club.

flames were free to race from the first floor to the third floor, causing the home to burn rapidly.

A ruptured gas line also helped to fuel the fire until Pacific Gas & Electric could arrive to shut it off, but that didn't happen until two in the morning. Pressurized tanks around the property were also exploding. Phoebe had every room wired for telephones and bells to ring for kitchen and valet service, leaving a labyrinth of wires running under the buildings. When interviewed the day after the fire, John Marshall confessed that efforts had been made to make the wiring safe, but he pointed out, "It was a complicated business." The air conditioner had been left on all day, and it was still running at 10:30 pm, allowing air to push through the duct system causing the fire to spread.

On the night of the fire, one of the fire chiefs made the statement that, "No water system would have saved the main structure." Ironically, a system of water hydrants

A large crane picks up remaining building debris and dumps it into a waiting truck to be hauled away. Massive toppled and broken pillars lay on the ground like fallen monarchs. The tree probably sustained damage and either survived or didn't. I'm not sure what the remaining building is ... perhaps the Music Room, the one part of the Hacienda that survived. Courtesy of Pleasanton's Museum on Main.

were being installed that were to be serviced by a reservoir near the sixteenth green. The following month in September 1969, the hydrants were scheduled to begin functioning. Larry Curtola stated that even these hydrants wouldn't have stopped the fire or saved the building. The bottom line was that there were no hydrants available to pump water to douse the flames. In desperation, Camp Parks (a nearby military training facility) was called to help drain the outdoor swimming pool of its 200,000 gallons. By two in the morning the pool was bone dry.

The day following the inferno, rumors and gossip began to fly as to the possible cause of the fire. Jon Frudden, Pleasanton Fire Chief, stated, "We may never know the real cause unless someone comes forward with a clearer story. The greenness of some of the firemen played a role in underestimating the size of the fire and how to properly attack it. In all, the men did their best. Every man gave his all at the fire and they are to be commended for a job well done." Chief Frudden went on to say that the

Carole MacRobert Steele

fire started in the north wing. Rooms were vacant, but there had been a Lions Club gathering there through Saturday night. It has been speculated that a cigarette could have been left smoldering on a rug or in an upholstered chair. The fact that the wiring was old and substandard was also considered as a possible cause. Livermore Fire Chief Jack Baird stated that, "The fire apparently started in a stairwell in the hotel room." This would be in keeping with what the night watchman had related to Terry Burt. The men who fought the fire were paid professionals, but volunteer firemen from surrounding communities also showed up to assist. With sparks floating half a mile into the air, the California Division of Forestry was called to keep the surrounding brush and grasslands from burning. Drifting embers spread to nearby luxury homes as scared homeowners used garden hoses to douse their roofs.

Piles of debris smoldered for three days as the curious and concerned came to view the ruins of the once grand estate. When the smoke cleared, all that remained was the music room, auxiliary buildings located at each end of the Hacienda, wrought iron grill work, twenty-nine red clay pots, and the famous Cellini gate, now warped and charred from the intense heat of the fire. The indoor pool, once covered over to make room for a bar when Prohibition ended, was now filled with the rubble of crumbled walls. Several days following the fire, Castlewood office staff toiled by the light of bare bulbs hanging in the music room, as they tried to straighten out the Club records that had fortunately been saved.

In summation, the Pleasanton Fire Department concluded that: An employee had tried to extinguish the fire without calling the fire department. The fire had been in progress for one to one-and-a-half hours before the alarm was turned in. The bartender had smelled smoke at 9:30 p.m. By the time the first engine arrived, the building was totally engulfed in flames.

As days passed, Club management felt an urgency to restore a sense of normalcy to its members as soon as possible. Ron Curtola, general manager, knew it was vitally important for functionality to be demonstrated in an effort to help close the gaping wound left by the devastating fire. With this in mind, the empty swimming pool was quickly refilled, and the sprinklers that had faithfully watered the lawns were turned back on. Minimal service was provided to members by reopening the men's locker room, and food was served in a makeshift eating area of the music room. It would be another year before any kind of dining facility would be available to the general public. Reflecting on the loss, Curtola stated, "You can't put a value on this place … the art, the architecture; everything about it is priceless." Castlewood was underinsured. It was a million-dollar loss with only $885,000 worth of coverage. The Club owed $353,000 on its monthly mortgage. The Castlewood Country Club

Postcard view of Castlewood Country Club as it appeared when it was rebuilt in the early 1970s, looking much the same today as it did forty-plus years ago. Caption on back reads: "Originally built for Phoebe Apperson Hearst, and completely rebuilt in the late 60's, this country club is set in beautiful surroundings and commands a spectacular view of Amador Valley." The publisher/printer got his facts and dates a little wrong!

Construction Committee began discussions about rebuilding, and the membership agreed, with reference to Phoebe, "We must reestablish the indomitable spirit of the Lady in Lavender and Lace, dedicated to gracious living exuding beauty of design and beauty in spirit."

John Marshall had his own ideas about how Castlewood should be rebuilt. The firm of Ratcliff, Slama & Cadwalader was hired to draw preliminary architectural plans for the new structure, estimated to cost $900,000. Marshall felt that Ratcliff's plan was "basically and fundamentally wrong." Castlewood's 400 members rejected Ratcliff's plan, believing that more than one plan should be considered before spending millions of dollars on reconstruction. So they asked John Marshall to review and make comments on the plan, which he did. He favored, "a building with the same general architectural style as the old clubhouse … Hispano-Moresque." However, some members didn't like Marshall's plan. One member claimed, "It appears to be a monument to the Hearsts." On the other hand, others believed that Ratcliff's design was not in keeping with "Castlewood tradition."

Marshall vehemently opposed some of Ratcliff's ideas for the new clubhouse,

This is the modern logo used by Castlewood Country Club. The castle represents the "castle" in Castlewood. The golf ball image shows the predominance of golf as a mainstay of the Club. The horse represents the period of time when Castlewood was well known for its superb polo fields and riding trails. The tree is for the oaks and sycamores on this heavily wooded property and might also represent the "wood" in Castlewood.

expressing his opinions as follows: "The old impressive clubhouse approach would be eliminated. The proposed design was "Monterey Modern" with a shopping center atmosphere in a sea of automobiles. Narrow corridors and a small lobby gives it an institutional feeling rather than a hospitable one. No allowances have been made for future building expansion. The members dining room and ballroom could not be joined together. The restrooms in the basement would be a source of irritation to non-golfers and visitors." Marshall went on to explain that the clubhouse should once again be a prestigious landmark with its outline of three towers visible from the valley. He wanted a covered passenger entrance for people to be able to exit their vehicles during inclement weather. He thought the circular driveway should be kept to retain as much of the old Hacienda feeling as possible. Marshall believed that adding a "Hearst Courtyard" would be appropriate; a brass plaque could be placed here, inscribed with words in tribute to Phoebe. In contrast, the Ratcliff plan called for the demolition of the courtyard and its walls; tearing them down would mean the loss of one of the few remaining Hearst and early Castlewood historic tie-ins.

Marshall wanted the clubhouse lobby to have an aura of elegance, dramatically affecting all who entered. As for the interior, he envisioned large paintings gracing the walls and artificial trees strategically placed in various spots round the room. He

Entrance sign on road leading into Castlewood, designed in keeping with the Spanish style of the original Hacienda and current Clubhouse

believed that the Cellini gate was salvageable and could be restored to its original grandeur, that it could be used as an impressive entrance into a cocktail lounge that could be named the "Cellini Bar." Cushioned perimeter seating could be installed in this bar, with a corner fireplace burning realistic-looking gas logs for added ambiance. To promote sociability, a u-shaped bar would allow patrons to sit across from each other. This arrangement would also help waiters to serve drinks in a more timely manner. The other bar in the clubhouse could be western-themed and named the "Comstock Bar," since George Hearst had acquired much of his wealth from the Comstock Lode in Nevada. In Marshall's opinion, having two bars built back-to-back would be a more efficient arrangement, providing for better storage of the liquor. Optimally, these measures would be more advantageous to both bartenders and customers. Marshall also proposed that a "Hearst Historical Room" be located in the clubhouse gallery to showcase memorabilia and artifacts from the Phoebe era. Over the years, several people asked Marshall about the history of the Hearsts, the Hacienda, and early Castlewood. It was his opinion that these items would be of tremendous interest to the general membership, and would allow visitors to learn about the illustrious Hearst family. He personally owned fifty photographs showing images taken during Phoebe's years at the Hacienda. He offered to display them

Carole MacRobert Steele

The road as it winds and climbs towards the causeway to Castlewood. Photo taken in 2003. The palms remain, but much of the original roadside foliage is gone, replanted with other less exotic plants. The cactus seen in this photo is not Burbank's spineless type.

on the walls of the new clubhouse, but he was reluctant to do so unless a sprinkler system was installed in case of a fire. In 1970, George Hearst, oldest son of William R. Hearst, expressed a desire to assist the Club in providing a "Hearst Historical Room." Even William R. Hearst, Jr. offered a donation from his foundation to help with the expense of developing such a room.

Marshall did not have kind words for the Ratcliff plan, calling it inflexible, impractical, and giving the new clubhouse a lack of distinction and personality. In a 1970 interview, Marshall stated, "This plan leaves something to be desired, in my opinion, from the standpoint of not taking full advantage of the choice building site, the breathtaking panoramic view of the valley below, the interrelationship of rooms and areas, convenience to members and staff, and cost and practicability of operation … and to make a mistake at this stage would be disastrous for all the foreseeable years to come." Marshall wanted to inspire beauty using the plan he'd developed, which was "simple, operationally practical, and easily understood." On February 26, 1970, after spending one-and-a-half months developing a completely new layout, Marshall submitted his plan to the Building Committee, Board of Directors, Trustees, and all 850 interested Club members, of which he was also a member and grounds resident.

Photo taken in 2003 showing ancient oaks and a paved path bordering the golf course.

Photo taken in 2003 shows the raised causeway leading to the Clubhouse with original palm trees and the swimming pool to the left.

Carole MacRobert Steele

This view of the lush setting and oak hills as seen from the Clubhouse looking back down the causeway. This view remains the same as it did in Phoebe's day. The palms Burbank planted still reign regal. Photo taken in 2003.

Photo of the Clubhouse entrance taken in 2003 shows the original clay pots dating from at least the 1969 fire. They are probably considerably older and possibly from Phoebe days.

First fairway taken in 2003 has changed very little from the late 1920s when it was constructed. The Clubhouse, not visible, is to the far left.

On March 5, 1970, Ratcliff was ultimately granted permission by the Alameda County Planning Commission to build the new clubhouse. On March 18, 1970, the drawings to build the 44,000 square foot property for an estimated $1.7 million were released for public viewing. In 1970, the Stolte Construction Company (which built the Oakland/Alameda coliseum) won the Castlewood bid. Construction on the concrete block structure was started in December, 1970. The new building would have a dining room, banquet room, kitchen, bars, and men's and women's locker rooms. With much fanfare and festivity, the day of the dedication finally arrived on March 5, 1972. In the new ballroom, members waltzed the night away in celebration. "Valleyites," who once referred to Castlewood as "the castle on the hill," would now gaze towards the hills and see only a large white building where once stood the towering Hacienda.

In 1991, renovation was done on the almost twenty-year old building. Eleven years later, in 2002, the property continued to show signs of wear and tear. Some members suggested tearing down the building and starting over, but doing that would have cost millions. In 2005, there were several areas of the property badly in need of repair or replacement: flooring and electrical components needed updating; the kitchen, administration offices, restrooms, lobby, and banquet room also needed modernizing and sprucing up. Four decades later, and with improvements made, the clubhouse is beautiful and looking pretty good for her age!

CHAPTER 7

SOME THINGS NEVER CHANGE

THE LAND NEVER CHANGES. THE OAK-STUDDED HILLS SIT AGAINST THE blue horizon. The palms on Castlewood Drive sway in the breeze, and the soil Phoebe walked upon is still part of the earth. Only the seasons change as the green hills of spring evolve into a colorful palette of orange, gold, and red in the autumn. The spirits that inhabited the Hacienda lost their home to fire, but one original building remains, one that Phoebe's eyes had seen. Proud of its past, it stands white and stately, though basically ignored, at the parking lot near the tennis courts.

In 2014, two Castlewood staff members gave me a tour of this musty old edifice that's currently being used as a storehouse for maintenance equipment, non-functioning golf carts, decades-old Christmas decorations, rusty cast iron patio chairs from days-gone-by, and other nonessential items. The dark and dank interior was illuminated only by daylight seeping through its crank-open glass windows protected by iron bars. Steep wooden stairs lead to the second floor of what had been living quarters for bachelors and servants during the Phoebe and Dude Ranch days. A row of wooden shower stall doors still swing on their creaking hinges. On the backside of this building is a small odd-looking box with the name Detex on it. Detex started business in 1878, and by 1928, it had become The Detex Corporation. It eventually became Detex Watchclock Corporation, which was the name we found on the box. Security guards used this mechanical clock as part of their property patrol system. The five-pound watchclock was carried in a leather pouch slung over the guard's shoulder. Detex watchclock stations consisted of a small metal box with a hinged lid. Inside the box was a numbered key affixed by a twelve-inch chain. The guard inserted the three-inch key into the lock, rotating it so that a time stamp would be pressed into a roll of paper inside the clock. This was the way in which each man on patrol knew what time each station had been checked. This watchclock security system was probably in place on all the original Hacienda buildings.

If the thick walls of this abandoned building could talk, what tales they could

2003 photo shows the only remaining original building from the Hacienda days, located on the Club parking lot. In previous decades it had been used as bachelor apartments and is now used for storage. On the back wall of this building is where we discovered the watchclock station.

With the metal lid lifted, this photo shows the watchclock station contents. The watchclock was used by the estate guards as they made their periodic daily security checks.

tell, what visions they had seen, what whispers they had heard, what secrets they still keep. So many decades have passed with so many souls harboring gaiety and trauma, sadness and laughter. Echoes of the past sail through its halls, catching a ride on the wind, carrying their messages back to Phoebe.

Casa Bonita can no longer tell its tales. Once located near the lower parking lot, the pink-colored Boys' House was still standing in 1978, but abandoned and vacant, leaving it vulnerable to vandals and teenage parties. The Club membership considered turning it into a professional building, offering deluxe office space for local merchants to lease. Unfortunately, it had sustained substantial water damage causing dry rot in the walls and windows. Repair and renovation was going to cost $500,000, and it was "just too expensive to save the old villa." Castlewood members voted to raze it rather than spend such a huge sum of money. A year later, in 1979, Casa Bonita was still vacant and deteriorating, and discussions commenced on turning it into a parking lot. Phoebe would have been crushed by this turn of events. The Amador-Livermore Valley Historical Society and the community joined forces to try and save the venerable old building from the wrecking ball by getting it designated as a California historical landmark, but all their efforts were in vain. After standing for seven decades, the beloved "beautiful house" was bulldozed in 1982, reduced to a rubble of fractured pink cement. In the end, Casa Bonita gave up its life to become a parking lot. The only items salvaged were old gates, door brass, and pieces from Spanish wrought iron chandeliers.

Castlewood, the elite private country club, lives on, having been resurrected from bankruptcy, the Great Depression, changes of ownership, and an all-consuming catastrophic fire. Castlewood thrives today because of its loyal members and world-class facilities. For decades it has served the public as a Statewide and hometown community institution because people are drawn to the unmatched beauty of its location. The Club strives to offer only the best in dining, personal and business entertaining, outdoor activities, and sports. It boasts one of the largest ballrooms in the Bay Area, easily accommodating dances, wedding receptions, and meetings of all sizes. Members delight in the social events held year-round, including several gala holiday celebrations.

Whether it's Phoebe's Hacienda, the dude ranch, or the country club, this land and its historic buildings have been entertaining members, guests, and locals for more than one hundred years. Phoebe would be extremely distraught that her house is gone forever, but she'd be happy knowing that good times continue. The thousands of people who visit her land are still her guests, and she's still the proud "Lady in Lavender," extending her hand in welcome.

I took this photo in 2003. This huge painting of Phoebe Hearst hung prominently in the Clubhouse lobby. When I returned in 2013, the painting was gone. There are various stories about its history. It may have belonged to Phoebe's late grand-nephew Bill Apperson of Pleasanton. The other story is that Castlewood Country Club paid thousands of dollars to commission the painting. Club members weren't fond of the painting, complaining that Phoebe's facial expression was too stern. For thousands of dollars more, the artist was hired to redo her expression to one that portrayed her with a softer look. The whereabouts of the painting are unknown as of this writing.

BIBLIOGRAPHY

Newsletters, Brochures, Pamphlets, Maps

California State Automobile Association. Bay and River Districts map Jan. 1949.

The Castlewood Country Club. 1920s brochure.

Castlewood Country Club. 2003 membership packet.

Castlewood Country Club. Meeting Our Needs – Realizing Our Potential. 2006 proposal.

Castlewood Country Club Executive Committee. Castlewood Country Club – Former Estate of Phoebe Apperson Hearst. 1926 membership booklet.

Howe, Denise & Amador-Livermore Valley Historical Society. Phoebe Apperson Hearst: The Pleasanton Years. 1986.

Old Hearst Ranch. 1950 brochure.

Rutherford, Tom. Castlewood Country Club Forecaster newsletter. "History of the Castlewood Country Club chapters 1-9, 2003.

Newspaper Articles

Agar, Joan. "Arrivederci, Castlewood!" *Tri-Valley Times,* August 31, 1969.

Bing, Jeb. "Bill Apperson: A Pleasanton Legacy." *Pleasanton Times,* February 25, 2005.

Buginas, Betty King. "Destruction Ends Hearst Ties." *The Valley Times,* July 13, 1982.

"Castlewood Shows New Look." *Pleasanton Times,* January 20, 1970.

"The Hearst Castle: Hacienda Del Pozo De Verona." *Pleasanton Times,* August 13, 1910.

"Hearst House Studied." *The Valley Times,* August 27, 1978.

Jacobs, Beth. "The Gardens." *The Daily Review,* October 16, 1977: Brightside Supplement.

Maloney, Sara. "Castlewood" and "The Clubhouse." *The Daily Review,* October 16, 1977 Brightside Supplement.

"Mary Frager's Memories of Champagne and Beer." *The Pleasanton Times,* April 9, 1969.

McNicoll, Ronald. "Castlewood Landmark." *The Valley Times,* July 13, 1982.

"Mrs. Phoebe Hearst Dies At Her Home in Pleasanton." *Sausalito News,* April 19, 1919.

"Mrs. Phoebe Hearst Seriously Ill at Hacienda." *Oakland Tribune,* February, 28, 1919.

"Old Castlewood Days." newspaper unknown, April 19, 1973.

"Prominent Pleasanton Man Dies." *The Daily Review,* February, 1976.

Schrader, Barry. "Hearst Pleasanton Ties Deep." *Oakland Tribune,* September 29, 2005.

Singleton, Jill. "Bulldozers Raze Hearst Home." *The Valley Times,* July 13, 1982.

Stevenson, Jen. "Phoebe Apperson Hearst." *Pleasanton Weekly,* April 13, 2001.

"The Story of a Fire – And a Second Disaster That Wasn't Meant To Be." *The Times,* August 27, 1969.

"Swimming Pool at Castlewood Club a Charmer." newspaper unknown, June 20, 1930.

Truebridge, Fen. "A Grand Lady Graced the Valley." *The Valley Times,* September, 19, 1979.

"Wedding Under Waving Palms." *Oakland Tribune,* September 15, 1903.

Winslow, Pete. "Hearst's Original Showplace Is Gone." *The Independent,* August 27,1969.

Books

Bonfils, Winifred Black, *The Life and Personality of Phoebe Apperson Hearst.* San Simeon, CA: Friends of Hearst Castle, 1991.

Boutelle, Sara Holmes, *Julia Morgan, Architect.* New York: Abbeville Press, 1995.

Coblentz, Edmond W*illiam Randolph Hearst: A Portrait in His Own Words.* New York: Simon and Schuster, 1952.

Coffman, Taylor, *Hearst Castle: The Story of William Randolph Hearst and San Simeon.* Santa Barbara, CA: Sequoia Communications, 1985.

Dunlap, John F, *The Hearst Saga: The Way It Really Was.* Medford, OR: John F. Dunlap, 2002.

Goldsmith, Bonnie, *William Randolph Hearst: Newspaper Magnate.* Edina, MN: ABDO Publishing Co., 2010.

Greenberg, Daniel, *Julia Morgan Architect.* New York: McGraw-Hill School Division, 1995.

Hearst, William Randolph, Jr., *The Hearsts: Father and Son.* Niwot, CO: Roberts Rinehart, 1991.

Levkoff, Mary L. *Hearst, The Collector.* New York: Harry N. Abrams, 2008.

Loe, Nancy E, *William Randolph Hearst: An Illustrated Biography.* San Simeon, CA: Aramark Leisure Services, 1988.

Luna, Henry and The Pacific Locomotive Association, *Images of Rail: Niles Canyon Railways.* San Francisco, CA: Arcadia Publishing, 2005.

Mayo, James M, *The American Country Club: Its Origins and Development.* New Brunswick, NJ: Rutgers University Press, 1998.

Nasaw, David, *The Chief: The Life of William Randolph Hearst.* New York: Houghton

Mifflin, 2000.

Older, Mrs. Fremont, *William Randolph Hearst: American*. New York: D. Appleton Century Company, 1936.

Procter, Ben, *William Randolph Hearst: The Early Years 1863-1910*. New York: Oxford University Press, 1998.

Robinson, Judith, *The Hearsts: An American Dynasty*. San Francisco: Telegraph Hill Press, 1991.

Swanberg, W. A, *Citizen Hearst*. New York: Galahad Books, 1961.

Tebbel, John, *The Life and Good Times of William Randolph Hearst*. New York: E. P. Dutton, 1952.

Wadsworth, Ginger, *Julia Morgan: Architect of Dreams*. Minneapolis: Lerner Publications, 1990.

Wainwright, Mary-Jo and the Museum on Main, *Images of America, Pleasanton*. San Francisco: Arcadia Publishing, 2007.

Whitelaw, Nancy, *William Randolph Hearst and the American Century*. Greensboro, NC: MorganReynolds, Inc., 2004.

Whyte, Kenneth, *The Uncrowned King: The Sensational Rise of William Randolph Hearst*. Berkeley, CA: Counterpoint Press, 2009.

Winslow, Carleton M, *The Enchanted Hill: The Story of Hearst Castle at San Simeon*. Los Angeles, CA: Rosebud Books, 1980.

ACKNOWLEDGEMENTS

I WISH TO EXPRESS MY THANKS BY ACKNOWLEDGING THOSE PEOPLE WHO helped make this book a reality.

From the very beginning, Debbie Leonardo, Director of Membership at Castlewood Country Club, was on board and eager to help me gather information on the history of Castlewood Country Club. She provided me with documents and photographs that have enabled me to present lesser-known information and images to interested readers. She was always prompt in answering my emails and willing to search through Castlewood archives stored "down in the basement." She and co-worker Kelly Derdak graciously gave their valuable time to take me on a tour of Castlewood in 2013. They granted me access to an original Hacienda building where the general public is not allowed. Kelly was most helpful in his knowledge about this building, which is now being used for storage.

Ken MacLennan, curator of the Museum on Main in Pleasanton, California, made available to me dozens of historic photographs depicting the Hacienda in its early days; as well as photos of Phoebe and her family. He has also written his own book on the history of Pleasanton. His staff of museum volunteers helped me sort through documents gleaned from the files pertaining to the Hacienda, Castlewood, and Old Hearst Ranch. Bless those volunteers for the time they give in helping us authors and researchers! The Museum on Main is worth a visit for those interested in Amador-Livermore Valley history.

This book wouldn't have been possible without the knowledgeable and talented staff at Luminare Press. Owner and editor Patricia Marshall assured me that she and her staff would be there every step of the way in getting this book to print...and they have been! My thanks to Patricia for heading up this project. George Filgate, of George Filgate Photography, did a superb job spending several hours photographing the images. Claire Flint Last, graphic designer, worked long and hard assembling the placement of the photos and text as they appear in the book. She came up with a cover design that was exactly the look I was hoping to achieve. I'm thankful to Jamie Passaro, who copyedited the book, for her knowledge of grammar and style. Having proofread this book dozens of times myself, I know what a tedious process it can be looking for errors that need correcting.

Last, but never least, I thank my husband Frank, who was always patient and encouraging through all the years and steps that it took to get this book written. He was my objective "second opinion" when it came to critiquing the book's text and images.